Alex

Happy Birthday, many thanks for your help with this!

Love

Bill

The Age of Disintegration

Bill Jordan

The Age of Disintegration

The Politics and Economics of Division

Bill Jordan
Exeter, UK

ISBN 978-3-030-41444-3 ISBN 978-3-030-41445-0 (eBook)
https://doi.org/10.1007/978-3-030-41445-0

This Palgrave Macmillan imprint is published by the registered company Springer Nature Switzerland AG.
The registered company address is: Gewerbestrasse 11, 6330 Cham, Switzerland

To the memory of Jean Packman, partner, colleague and inspiration

Acknowledgements

For helpful discussions and suggestions, I would like to thank Sarah Jordan, Linda and Colin Janus-Harris, Alexandra Allan and John Ingham.

Contents

CHAPTER 1

Introduction

Abstract The collective life of human beings has alternated between periods of enlargement in units (from tribes to empires and federations) to fragmentation. At a local level, the recent history has been the substitution of private collective services for state-run ones. Now the new era of globalisation and automation has brought problems in the maintenance of collective institutions of all kinds.

Keywords Automation • Globalisation • Human collectives

Human collectives are enormously diverse in size and composition; they also rely on a number of different mechanisms, processes and factors for their creation and maintenance. For centuries, they were units for the survival of our ancestors, who lived in small family groups, within larger tribes, sustained by beliefs about natural and supernatural forces. A series of systems of rule by those who seized ownership of the land and created laws on property rights, states and empires, and eventually superstates like the USA, the USSR and China, constituted stable or shifting units, often in conflict, either internally or against each other.

Is it possible to generalise about the likely future viability of any of these collective units (from families to superstates) in the face of present-day technological, economic and social change? In this book, I shall explore these questions, starting from the proposition that long-standing

B. Jordan, *The Age of Disintegration*,
https://doi.org/10.1007/978-3-030-41445-0_1

collective structures, and the institutions which sustain them, are simultaneously under pressure from these forces and are already in the process of re-formation, even as they disintegrate.

The twentieth century was a particularly traumatic one for large-scale collectivities. The Austrian, Spanish and British Empires were beginning to break up during the first two decades, contributing to the onset of the disastrous First World War. Hitler's imperialist ambitions brought about the Second World War and accelerated the access to national self-rule among British colonies in Asia and Africa, as well (after wars of independence) as those of Portugal and France, while still consolidating the power of the Soviet Union, which had suffered the largest human toll during the war.

So in the West the tendency was towards national autonomy, and this was greatly enhanced by the break-up of the USSR. But there was also, of course, the emergence of new, quasi-federal unions of states, in Europe and (in a weaker form) in Africa and Asia, as national governments sought to shelter from the disruptive impact of global economic forces on the protective institutions through which they had contrived to shield them.

But at the same time, within these national and transnational collective units, the collectivities which had structured their economies and societies were crumbling. Long-standing organisations, from trades unions to civil societies' voluntary organisations, were losing members, as a culture of individualism, home ownership and consumerism seemed to dispense with the need for these protections. All this was slightly later paralleled by the decline in support for traditional Conservative (Christian Democratic) and Labour (Social Democratic) political parties and the rise of Green and radical Right-Wing ones.

This book will argue that the disintegration of historical collective bodies threatens the fabric of our social order and could lead to dangerous conflicts. The rise of authoritarian leaders (such as Donald Trump, Boris Johnson and Viktor Orbán) could trigger the emergence of 'mass societies', which are intolerant, exclusionary and coercive towards minorities, including poor people. But this is not inevitable; I shall propose ways in which these trends could be reversed, and a more tolerant, equal and inclusive order established.

Smaller or Larger Collectives?

In his book *In Care of the State*, Abram de Swaan (1988) argued that it was issues of poverty and its management that led to the collectivisation of administrations, on a larger and larger scale, and ultimately to welfare states. Whereas political authority was primarily concerned with law, justice and social control on the one hand, and military defence and aggression on the other (Mann 1980), these collective arrangements expanded to include provision for education, health, social care services and environmental controls.

So the overall tendency of these processes was towards both larger collective units and the professionalisation of tasks previously (for the vast majority of citizens) supplied by family members or local village elders. But first, as there were inevitably limits in the extent to which large political units could effectively provide and regulate such services, and professional bodies guarantee their quality, at some point, there was bound to be resistance to the internationalisation of what had been tasks central to nation states and to the penetration of international commercial bodies into services which defined the sense of membership and political belonging (such as the British NHS). So it was not so much a question of one set of collectivities being replaced by another, as of the maintenance of all forms of solidarity becoming problematic over the same period (or so it seemed).

Yet it is clearly the case that all forms of human collectivities have boundaries (physical borders, economic charges and fees, or social signifiers) which include members and exclude non-members. As globalisation has eroded the boundaries of nation states and their constituent organisations, it has also widened the scope of other kinds of collectivities, as commercial bodies, many of them international in reach, have come to supply the services formerly organised by states. This process has accelerated transnational movement of staff, such as doctors and nurses, and eroded political controls over the nature and quality of the services, eligibility for them and the rules governing national borders.

One obvious manifestation of these phenomena has been the Brexit farago. Since the referendum of 2016 (itself an ill-judged response by Prime Minister David Cameron to the rise of populist nationalism in England and to the growth of support for Scottish independence), there has been a furious dispute about the UK's future, crystalised in the inability to find an agreed formula for leaving the EU. In all this, the almost equal division of seats in the House of Commons after the 2017 election gave exaggerated power to the ten Democratic Unionist MPs, themselves representatives of barely half the Northern Ireland electorate. It also gave disproportional significance to the Irish border issue, as a determinant of whether Britain could leave with a deal to avoid catastrophic effects on trade with the EU. The Democratic Unionist Party (DUP) argued that the proposed deal potentially violated the terms of the Good Friday agreement, which had sustained peace in Ireland for 21 years. The election of December 2019 resulted in a large Conservative majority, but the fact that nationalist parties made gains in both Scotland and Northern Ireland sufficient to give them a majority in favour of remaining in the EU exacerbated the problems of the Union.

So borders—and especially the shifting implications of borders for political and economic issues—took on a significance at this time that was unprecedented for any period of UK history since the seventeenth century, as the governments of Theresa May and Boris Johnson, despite their very different political affiliations and loyalties, both struggled unsuccessfully to achieve majorities for any compromise. They were as much rendered impotent by divisions within their own parties as by any unified opposition, another example of the process of fragmentation that is characteristic of the present age.

A further instance is that of Spain and the saga over the secession of Catalonia. The five leaders of the 'coup' that followed the referendum on independence for the province who had remained in the country were each sentenced to between 9 and 13 years of imprisonment on 13 October 2019, provoking days of demonstrations by Catalans. But even these demonstrators were almost equally divided between those prepared to use violence and those who wanted peaceful mass protests; from his exile in Belgium, their former leader, Carlos Puigemont, pleaded for non-violent action.

These examples suggest that the root causes of the new wave of disintegration in political units are new priorities in the sense of collective belonging—cultures of national or regional loyalty that move members of such communities to join with like-minded others to assert their identities in protests, or to vote for parties representing such views. But at the individual level, it also indicates that citizens experience themselves as members of these smaller collectives, even when they purchase and consume commodities and experiences from all over the world, their work and leisure may involve travel abroad, and when they receive electronic communications and watch films and TV from every continent.

So, individual consciousness seems to have moved in the direction of less binding affiliations and fewer organisational memberships; but at the same time towards a less universal (or international) type of affiliation, as if economic uncertainties and insecurities have contributed to the need to belong to a more traditional, familiar type of collective entity.

This refocusses attention on the processes by which collectives are bound together—the emotional and intimate, the associational and co-operative, and those that stem from organisational membership and belonging. In this book, I shall explore why all of these, in their different ways, are being eroded and weakened.

This process began, of course, when influential US economists like J.M. Buchanan (1965, 1968) presented models of collective action which analysed it solely in terms of the quantifiable advantages they gave to individuals and argued that these gains could be more reliably achieved through exclusive collectivities of those who shared particular risks and could afford the fees ('clubs'), rather than aggregating large populations, including those with the highest risk factors and least able to contribute (low earners and people with long-term illnesses and disabilities), and supplied by public (state) agencies (health and social care systems). It was the application of these principles, through privatisation of services, that led to the 'Great Exclusion'—the increased isolation, stigmatisation and coercion of the most disadvantaged members of societies (Jordan 1996).

The point here was that, while depreciating the value of membership and belonging stemming from larger-scale, inclusive collectivities (communities, nations), this dominance of market-orientated economic logics also weakened the ties of intimacy, affection, community and association; the commercialisation of organisations such as co-operatives and friendly societies re-enforced this cultural shift. Even if citizens did not actively embrace the new cult of individual achievement, property ownership and self-responsibility, or the organisations that enabled its practices, they were necessarily influenced by them. I have only to compare the world in which I grew up (in the 1940s to the 1960s) with that in which my children did (the 1970s to the 1990s) to recognise how much this shift influenced choices of careers, lifestyles and relationships.

These changes in the fundamental nature of membership and belonging in Western societies, experienced even more suddenly and traumatically in the former Soviet-dominated countries and in China, have now (after a generation) come under new transformative pressures from the loss of security of employment and income that accompanied technological innovation (automation and Artificial Intelligence). Without the protections of post-war welfare states or class-based professional or trades union organisations, they now face new insecurities and risks, because they may no longer be able to afford private insurance or membership of commercial collective services.

A clear example of this is the case of social care in the UK. It is extremely expensive, especially when elderly and disabled people reach the stage of needing residential provision; yet repeated attempts by successive governments to reform the system for financing it have failed, or covered only a small minority of those in need. Because collective provision has been left to private insurance companies and commercial organisations for care services, all but the poorest citizens are left to their own devices at the time of their lives when they are most vulnerable; they have to run down their resources until they qualify. The unreformed state of social care also contributed to a situation where there was a 75 per cent increase in patients returning to hospital after discharge in the 10 years to 2017 (BBC Radio 4, *Today*, 3 December 2017). Life expectancy has also ceased to rise in the UK and declined in poor districts (Radio 4, '*Life Expectancy*', 10 September 2019).

But a more drastic case of collective systems failure in this sphere has been Japan's. Although it prides itself on the paternalism of its large companies and its pension schemes, these have covered a decreasing proportion of citizens in recent years, causing a drastic form of insecurity, especially for older divorced and widowed men. This was signalled by an extraordinary increase in the incidence of minor criminality, mainly shoplifting, among older men, which has resulted in a rapid growth in prison populations of offenders aged over 60. Since overall crime rates in Japan are low by international standards, this was especially striking; it is now apparent that these older men became unable to look after themselves or manage their diminished resources, and had committed such minor offences repeatedly, in order to be looked after in prison, because social care was much too expensive for them to afford.

Japanese prison regimes are authoritarian, consisting of drilling, boot-camp routines, and shouted orders by officers. However, they have been forced to adapt to the fact that over one-fifth of the inmates are now over 60 and many are disabled (BBC Radio 4, '*Crossing Continents*', 17 January 2019).

The Significance of Collective Systems Failures

How significant have the failures of collective systems been for the lives of citizens of developed societies and how—if at all—have they contributed to the rise of populism, nationalism and authoritarianism? These are very large and complex questions, which I shall attempt to address in this book.

The main point for this introduction is that the period in which individual citizens of these countries—the years covered by the Thatcher and Blair leaderships in the UK, and the Reagan, Bush and Clinton presidencies in the USA—was one of increased inequality (on many dimensions) among populations, and of the emergence of impoverished and excluded communities of disadvantaged, many of minority ethnic people. These in turn resisted against their situations and in some districts by various kinds of deviant behaviour—working while claiming, drug abuse, criminality, family break-up and mental illness (Jordan et al. 1992). These communities were coerced and sanctioned by the benefits authorities (Haagh 2019a), as well as harassed by the police and controlled by the social services.

It seems as if this produced a delayed political reaction in these societies. Over the following 10 years or so, a growing number of people turned away from the established political parties in the UK and in Europe, and towards Far-Right ones, or (to a lesser extent) the Greens. Above all, some who were not poor or disadvantaged to the extent of the excluded class, but whose insecurity of employment and variable earnings made them feel acutely at risk of falling into that class, became both anxious and angry about their situation. These were the *Gilets Jaunes* in France who besieged President Macron, but they were also often those who supported the rise of President Trump and voted for other Far-Right parties in Europe, including Hungary, where Viktor Orbán came to power.

What populist nationalist leaders seemed to promise these citizens was recognition as authentic, valued and *definitive* members of their regional and national communities, whose claims to such recognition had been denied by liberal democrats and democratic socialists, and besmirched by mass immigration from the Middle East, Asia and Africa. For many, the symbols of these outsiders were the new waves of Roma gypsies—always present as small minorities in Western Europe, but established in larger numbers in Hungary and Eastern Slovakia. In Trump's USA, of course, the immigrants were from Central and South America, and their symbols were Mexicans.

So, it was primarily the failure of systems for managing migration (Jordan and Duevell 2003) which fed into this resentment, and in many cases supplied its slogans and rallying cries. But it was the threat of rapid economic change, caused by the combination of globalisation (outward investment and relocation of industrial production) and the impact of new technologies (originally robotics, but most recently artificial intelligence

(AI), leading to the automation of many service activities) which threatened their very identities. In this book, I shall analyse how populist, nationalist politicians mobilised and harnessed their anxiety and anger, and also gained support from older people, nostalgic about the past age of a society structure around industrial production, trades unions and working-class civil society organisations and identifying with protesters' resentments.

Disintegration of the collective bodies symbolically represented by Conservative (Christian Democratic) and Socialist (Social Democratic) political parties was, therefore, a delayed reaction to economic and social change, which had been progressing over decades. This had largely been denied expression in the period of economic austerity which followed the financial crash of 2007–2008, and it now burst out, coming as a shock to the traditional political parties, which had complacently assumed that they had 'managed' that crisis and its long and painful aftermath. Instead they found that resentment and the sense of insecurity had been simmering, especially in those districts most affected by globalisation, and most threatened by the prospect of automation, and those most resentful about the relative economic success of refugee populations, often consisting mainly of middle-class, educated people (Jordan 2019a, b).

The disintegration of collectivities accelerated by globalisation and new technologies is unlikely to be significantly slowed by the policies of populist nationalist leaders. Ironically, of course, Donald Trump himself is an iconic global capitalist, with enterprises (and golf courses) all over the world; these are of much greater economic significance than his token attempts to revive rust-belt US industrial districts, or to build walls for the exclusion of those who migrate on foot from South and Central America.

If national political collective units are becoming more difficult to sustain, a surprising reversal of long-term decline has been the revival of religion as a focus for collective action. This began, of course, when the 'Arab Spring' of 2011 was followed, not so much by the rise of democratic regimes but by mass mobilisations of Islamic faith collectives. Here the fundamentalist militancy of Islamic State, with its ruthless campaign of mass murder, and the mobilisations inspired by the Iranian regime, leading to the civil war in Yemen and the continuing conflict in Syria, all ensured that the Middle East remained a zone of social conflict. Collectivities were set against each other in an age of chaotic warfare rather than political disintegration.

At the same time, the rise to power of Narendra Modi in India showed that there, too, majorities could be mobilised around resentment against religious minorities. Although this was not the kind of phenomenon witnessed in the Middle East, it did resemble the mobilisations in the West, such as that of Donald Trump, in emphasising that national identity coincided with a particular individual identity, in this case, the one represented by the Hindu faith.

So the fragmentation of collectives occurred at many different levels and around diverse economic and social characteristics; equally, the re-formation of new collectives resulted in a diversity of parties, organisations and associations. Disintegration affected a wide range of long-standing collective bodies, some hundreds of years old; many of the new organisations were filling gaps left by these, others were meeting entirely new needs and purposes.

The Science of Disintegration

We would not, as social scientists, expect that the processes of disintegration and re-integration would be likely to have parallels in the world of nature and the scientific laws governing the universe; but in fact they do. The very eminent scientist, John Scales Avery, author of *Information Theory and Evolution* (2003) and *Civilization's Crisis: A Set of Linked Challenges* (2017), explains this in terms of the relationship between 'entropy' (disorder) and the order of the world (and universe) as we perceive them (*Countercurrents*, 15.3.2017).

He says that the earth is not a closed system; a flood of information-containing energy reaches the earth's biosphere in the form of sunlight. Although the second law of thermodynamics asserts that entropy in the universe must always increase, and hence the universe must always be moving towards greater disorder, so as to create a local order (e.g. on earth), disorder must be exported to the universe as a whole, thus increasing the total amount of disorder overall.

The information in sunlight is largely degraded as heat, but part of it is converted into cybernetic information and preserved in the complex structures of life. Natural selection ensures that, once this occurs, 'the configurations of matter in living organisms increase in complexity, refinement and statistical improbability. This is the process we call evolution, or in the case of human society, progress' (J.S. Avery, interview with B. Mathew, *Countercurrents*, p. 4).

He speaks of 'society's explosive accumulation of information and knowledge', accelerating to a point where 'it threatens to shake society to pieces', so that 'neither social institutions, nor political structures, nor education, nor public opinion can keep pace. The lightning-like pace of technical progress has made many of our ideas and institutions obsolete. For example, the absolutely sovereign nature of nation states and the institutions of war have both become dangerous anachronisms in an era of instantaneous communication, global interdependence and all-destroying weapons' (p. 5).

As Schrödinger states in his *What Is Life?* (1944), 'the device by which an organism maintains itself at a fairly high level of orderliness ... really consists of sucking orderliness from its environment'. Avery thought that environmental stress and destructive weapons were greater threats because this disorder is now global in scale; this means that only through a single, co-operative society, bolstered by education and religion, can the world be saved.

Meanwhile, of course, economic theory has become the dominant rationale for the political and social spheres of human organisation, and it has only fitfully paid attention to the concept of entropy. Frederick Soddy, who won the Nobel Prize for Chemistry in 1926 (in co-operation with Rutherford) thought that free energy was connected with wealth, but only tenuously with money. He criticised the banking system and recognised that crises like the sub-prime one of 2008 and debt one of 2011 demonstrated the second law of thermodynamics; as entropy increases, real wealth decays, whereas compound interest increases exponentially without limit. In his *Wealth, Virtual Wealth and Debt* (1926), he therefore anticipated the Crash and Great Depression. In the same vein, Nicholas Georgescu-Roegen (1971) a Romanian mathematician, saw how entropic transformation of valuable natural resources with low entropy, such as oil and good soil, could be turned into valueless waste with high entropy by human over-exploitation (*The Entropy Law and Economic Progress*).

Herman C. Daly (1991) followed this up with his advocacy of *The Steady-State Economy*, Washington, DC: Island Press, in which growth in the economic sub-system is balanced with the ecosphere's (total system's) metabolic throughput—too-rapid economic growth means the earth can no longer provide either sources or sinks that are needed. Furthermore, because eco-systems are complex (unlike the laws of physics), interactions between the activities of species are unpredictable—as in the mid-eighteenth century extinction of a type of sea-cow, as a result of the decline in populations of North American sea-otters (through human fur-hunting), which in turn had fed on molluscs that cut free the sea-kelp on which the sea-cows fed (BBC Radio 4, '*Extinctions*', 7 November 2019).

All these ideas were deployed to explain uneven development in the world's economies. The developing countries had been induced to borrow sums which by the 1970s represented crippling debts, sums which their leaders had spent mainly on armaments, and the creditor (developed) nations' authorities used these to extract raw materials without debt-reduction. Within affluent societies, concentrations of wealth-holdings by powerful oligarchs, who exploited tax loopholes and controlled government policies, all contributed to growing inequalities among citizens.

These authors argued that it was therefore essential to adapt all human institutions, since the nation states which still commanded military hardware and negotiated international relations through their threat power were perilously anachronistic in a new world linked together through digital technology. Somehow a more appropriate ethical framework, based on affiliation to the whole human race, must replace these legacies from the primitive, tribal past. They proposed that the social media, which played an ever-growing part in the lives of people everywhere, should be central to this.

Taking up the Hungarian-American physiologist and chemist Albert Szent-Gyorgyi's insight that, since information is central to the development and functioning of societies, and the depletion of fossil fuels, climate change, the refugee crisis, loss of solidarity and the rise of populist authoritarianism are all linked, the fact that the human mind appears to have been designed for gaining advantage in the competitive world of our primitive ancestors is potentially disastrous for humanity and the planet.

Solar-energy-based power is the only viable foundation for future sustainability (Stayton 2019), so investment in renewables is essential to ward off catastrophe. Science can provide such solutions, but not the political and social movements to fund and implement them. Life, even in peaceful and sustainable human societies, has always been precarious, since it is easier to destroy than to build for survival, to kill than to educate. Statistics, therefore, favour chaos over order—the 'Butterfly effect'.

In all these ways, therefore, scientists have quite independently provided a theoretical account of the disorder that is evident in the political and economic spheres in the present age. It suggests that there is a scientific basis for the theory of alternation between periods of stability and growth, followed by recession and conflict, first advanced by Karl Polanyi

(1944). He analysed these as 50-year cycles, the recessionary and conflictual one in his lifetime having been from the First World War to the Second. But if anything these cycles have accelerated; the collapse of the Soviet Union and the growth spurt of the 1990s was followed by the financial crisis less than 20 years later.

It has been, perhaps, the impact of the information revolution (Artificial Intelligence, automation) that has brought about this acceleration. But it is certainly not the only factor. Religion has not brought humankind together; it seems, especially in the rise of Muslim fundamentalism, mobilised in Islamic State, to have cast populations back into the era of the medieval crusades or the wars between Catholics and Protestants in sixteenth- and seventeenth-century Europe.

Capitalism and Political Collectivities

The study of disintegration and re-integration must try to find a way to analyse how the financial system, with its cycles of lending, debt and bankruptcy, maps onto the political chart of nation states and larger federations and unions. Ever since the Bretton Woods agreement at the end of the Second World War, this has involved shifts and crises; there can be no permanent, or even long-term solutions to the search for optimal correspondence between these two very diverse systems, because both are, in their own ways, inherently unstable.

The post-war world was prodded and prompted by the dominant Western ally, the United States, into a set of linked political relationships, partly in response to the threat posed by the Soviet Union. At Stuttgart in 1946, the US Secretary of State, James F. Byrnes, delivered his 'Speech of Hope', offering Germany the opportunity to join the other 'peace-loving nations', not only as a member of the United Nations, but also in the embryonic European Community. Initially, the financial collective unit was called the 'dollar zone', and it aimed to maintain monetary stability through fixed exchange rates, and to use budgetary surpluses in some countries to bail out deficits if others ran into trouble, through the International Monetary Fund (IMF).

By the early 1960s, a version of this plan was actually working, through co-ordination between central bankers of many nations, and enabled by the ever-widening and deepening political links constructed in the European Community. For instance, the French trade deficit with Germany, constantly putting pressure on the Banque de France to devalue the franc, led the German Bundesbank and those of other surplus nations to defend the franc, so long as they believed it to be viable, and so long as the USA was in surplus with the rest of the non-communist world (Varoufakis 2016, pp. 27–31).

However, in 1971, the USA expelled the European nations from the dollar zone. The US trade surplus with Europe had become a deficit, as European (and Japanese) productivity had overtaken that of America. Eventually, after various false starts, the Europeans were able to create a common currency, the euro, though the UK, which had only recently joined the Community, did not adopt this. But it also turned out that the euro was not proof against global financial crises, as was proved by the events of 2008.

Varoufakis argues that Europe never really recovered from the crisis that started with the collapse of the bank Northern Rock in the UK, and then enveloped Greece, which had no state funds left to cope with its insolvent central bank's problems, and all of whose citizens paid the price for the folly of its 'inane bankers' (p. 5); with Ireland suffering much the same fate, Portugal, Spain, Italy and Cyprus soon followed.

All this accelerated the processes by which the least advantaged in these societies became reliant on very poorly paid service work, mostly subsidised by means-tested state payments, into which they were driven by the authorities (Jordan 2019a, b; Haagh 2019a, b). The dreams of post-war welfare states in the developed economies, and of those Southern European countries which were growing faster in the 1970s and 1980s, were all dashed, as Europe became more like the USA, in terms of its inequalities, lack of security of income or the protection of state services against contingencies of ill health and accidents and the absence of a vision for positive transformation and progress.

So collective life in all these countries at the national and international levels mirrored the shift in principles for membership of economic organisations and civil society associations in their constituent societies (as citizens' inclusive state protections were dissolved and better-off individuals gained opportunities for gaining advantages by joining exclusive schools and health-care providers) and further enabled these through changes in their own configurations. The financial crash greatly re-enforced the effects of these political transformations, as the troubled downward decades of one of Polanyi's (1944) counter-cycles in his account of capitalism's alternation between growth and recession set in, and many were left facing insecure and fearful futures.

The implications of these developments, in terms of integration and disintegration, were in large part captured by Hirschman's (1970) analysis of collectives in terms of 'exit, voice and loyalty'. What public-choice theorists like Buchanan, and more particularly Mancur Olson (1982), discussed but could not possibly have predicted was the way in which the transformations of all collectives that their ideas incorporated in the 1980s and 1990s led to whole new configurations of the nations of the globe. Not only was there the spectacular dissolution of the former Soviet Union into separate states in Central Asia; within all the major national units which had been consolidated into states from the sixteenth to the nineteenth centuries (Spruyt 1994), there were pressures from their regions for various degrees of autonomy, some of which were successful in achieving full independent status. Exit increased, loyalty decayed.

In his book *Upheaval: How Nations Cope with Crisis and Change*, Jared Diamond (2019) analysed how states which had experienced the trauma of a period of murderous, dictatorial rule (Finland, Chile, Indonesia, Japan and Germany) could learn from each other's experiences, take responsibility and compromise for the sake of better futures. The scale of some of these slaughters had been enormous (Indonesia's military dictators had killed half a million citizens, Hitler's Germany many times that number), and some were still in a state of denial about their leaders' past atrocities (for instance, Japan's reluctance to allow foreign immigration and its lengthy failure to recall its massacres in China and Korea); but to varying degrees, all had managed to come to terms with their pasts.

So both disintegration and re-integration of collective bodies have been enduring features of the histories of human relationships at all levels; but each age has been characterised by a predominant form of institutions (empires, nation states or economic unions, for instance), and some ages have seen more radical transformations than others. The aim of this book is to clarify the nature of the transition that we are experiencing now, with particular reference to the tendency of certain types of collective to break up, and of populist, nationalist authoritarianism to become a more marked feature of political mobilisations, and in some cases governments.

I shall not pretend to be able to predict the likely duration or consequences of this stage in the evolution of human collectives. This has been far too complex, and the influence of changes at the largest and the smaller, communal level too varied, to reach any conclusion of this kind. But there does seem to be evidence that certain kinds of collective bodies, particularly nation states and unions of such polities, are still experiencing a period of disintegrative pressures, both from economic globalisation and from internal collective action by their citizens. The interaction between these two factors will be the focus of my analysis in this book.

References

Avery, J. S. (2003). *Information Technology and Evolution*. London and Singapore: World Science Publishing.

Avery, J. S. (2017). *Civilization's Crisis: A Set of Linked Challenges*. London and Singapore: World Science Publishing.

Buchanan, J. M. (1965). An Economic Theory of Clubs. *Economica, 32*, 1–14.

Buchanan, J. M. (1968). *The Demand and Supply of Public Goods*. Chicago: Rand McNally.

Daly, H. C. (1991). *The Steady-State Economy*. Washington, DC: Island Press.

Diamond, J. (2019). *Upheaval: How Nations Cope with Crisis and Change*. London: Allen Lane.

Georgescu-Roegen, N. (1971). *Entropy and Economic Progress*. Cambridge, MA: Harvard University Press.

Haagh, L. (2019a). *The Case for Universal Basic Income*. Cambridge: Polity.

Haagh, L. (2019b). Public State Ownership with Varieties of Capitalism: Regulatory Foundations foe Welfare and Freedom. *International Journal of Public Policy, 15*(2), 153–184.

Hirschman, A. O. (1970). *Exit, Voice and Loyalty: Responses to Decline in Firms, Organisations and States*. Cambridge, MA: Harvard University Press.

Jordan, B. (1996). *A Theory of Poverty and Social Exclusion*. Cambridge: Polity.

Jordan, B. (2019a). *Authoritarianism and How to Counter It*. London: Palgrave Macmillan.

Jordan, B. (2019b). *Automation and Human Solidarity*. London: Palgrave Macmillan.

Jordan, B., & Duevell, F. (2003). *Irregular Migration: The Dilemmas of Transnational Mobility*. Cheltenham: Edward Elgar.

Jordan, B., James, S., Kay, H., & Redley, M. (1992). *Trapped in Poverty? Labour Market Decisions in Low-Income Households*. London: Routledge.

Mann, M. (1980). State and Society, 1130–1815: An Analysis of English State Finances. In M. Zeitlin (Ed.), *Political Power and Social Theory* (Vol. 1, pp. 180–209). Delhi: Jai Press.

Olson, M. (1982). *The Rise and Decline of Nations: Economic Growth, Stagflation and Social Rigidities*. New Haven, CT: Yale University Press.

Polanyi, K. (1944). *The Great Transformation: The Political and Economic Origins of Our Time*. Boston, MA: Beacon Press.

Schrödinger, A. (1944). *What Is Life?* Cambridge: Cambridge University Press.

Soddy, F. (1926). *Wealth, Virtual Wealth and Debt.* London: Allen and Unwin.
Spruyt, H. (1994). *The Sovereign State and Its Competitors: An Analysis of Systems Change.* Princeton, NJ: Princeton University Press.
Stayton, R. (2019). *Solar Dividends: How Solar Energy Can Generate a Basic Income for Everyone on Earth.* Santa Cruz, CA: Chronos.
Swaan, A. de. (1988). *In Care of the State: Health Care, Education and Welfare in Europe and the USA in the Modern Era.* Cambridge: Polity.
Varoufakis, Y. (2016). *And the Weak Suffer What They Must? Europe, Austerity and the Threat to Global Stability.* London: Bodley Head.

CHAPTER 2

National and Regional Autonomy

Abstract All over the world, established political units are coming under pressure from movements for independence of their constituent nations or regions. Within the exit of the UK from the European Union, there is the campaign for Scottish independence and the continuing strife over Northern Ireland; Catalonia wants independence from Spain, Hong Kong from China and Russian minorities from Ukraine and the Baltic states, to say nothing of the seemingly endless conflicts in Syria, now also involving Turkey. This chapter will seek to explain the issues of disintegration at stake in these struggles.

Keywords Disintegration • Regional autonomy • National boundaries • Self-rule

For most of recorded history, powerful rulers sought to extend their territories by conquest of others, to colonise or subjugate these conquered peoples and to set up their own systems of law and means of extracting wealth. Nation states became established in the sixteenth and seventeenth centuries (Spruyt 1994), but they vied with empires, which rose and fell during the next 300 years. In the nineteenth century, one of these empires, the Ottoman, was in decline, and many of its provinces gained independence; by the beginning of the twentieth, another, the Austro-Hungarian, was also crumbling, and the First World War was sparked by the

B. Jordan, *The Age of Disintegration*,
https://doi.org/10.1007/978-3-030-41445-0_2

assassination of the Emperor's heir by a Serbian nationalist. The Second World War was a direct consequence of the imperialist ambitions of Hitler's Germany, Mussolini's Italy and the Ministers serving the Emperor of Japan. So, empires and their decline seemed to have spawned first disintegration, as new states emerged, and then the attempt of dictatorships to re-establish such transnational regimes. The Second World War led to a resumed round of disintegration, either through the militancy of national independence movements, or—as in the case of some of the British Empire after the war—because the colonial power chose to give them their autonomy.

Rivalry between the Soviet Union and the USA complicated this process, most notably in the case of the French colonies in Indo-China; but by the 1980s, it seemed that an orderly disintegration of the colonial empires of the European powers had been at last achieved, and this was followed in the early 1990s by the disintegration of the USSR. In place of these supranational political units, mainly economic unions of the EU, and comparable if less binding unions in Africa and East Asia, appeared to be the political counterparts of globalisation (the internationalisation of investment, production and trade). Although the Middle East was still a trouble-spot, financial crises seemed to have replaced political ones as the chief source of disruption; even notoriously long drawn-out conflicts like the one in Northern Ireland appeared to have been resolved.

Now suddenly there are assertions of independence and bids for autonomy on every continent. Scottish nationalism has become the dominant force in that country, and Northern Irish re-assertion of its sovereignty has disrupted the UK's bid to extricate itself from the European Union, itself a step towards disintegration. Catalonia's attempt at self-rule has been ruthlessly put down by Spain; Russian and Hungarian concentrations in Ukraine have bid for autonomy, as have Russians in Estonia; and in Hong Kong, lengthy mass demonstrations have resisted integration into China. Unrest in Venezuela has spilled over into Central America, contributing to the conflict between some provinces of Mexico and its government, and leading to oppressive incarceration of refugees by the US authorities. Riots and protests over poverty against the Chilean government occurred in some districts in October 2019. These peaked with a demonstration by over a million citizens against the regime, sparked by a small rise in the price of Metro tickets in the capital.

On 24th of that month, in addition to the continuing Chilean unrest, there were fresh demonstrations in Lebanon demanding the resignation of the government coalition (which included former warlords), accusing all its members of corruption, and demanding investment to repair its shattered utilities and transport infrastructure (Radio 4, *News*). Meanwhile, the Democratic Unionist Party in Northern Ireland was making threats of 'public disorder' on the streets if it did not get specific guarantees about its concerns over the latest version of the Brexit deal.

In this chapter, I shall analyse why there seems to have been a recent increase in disputes and conflicts about the boundaries of nationality and the autonomy of regions. Some of these are old issues flaring up again (as in Lebanon); others are ones that have been simmering for a while and now come back to the boil (as in Northern Ireland); and others still are relatively new (as in the Russian minorities in the newly independent countries of the former Soviet Union). But all relate to the balance between a number of factors which make up the adhesive or aggregating forces in any society. As this balance shifts, some kinds of order may become more fragile and some kinds of disorder increase.

Explanations of Order in Polities

Hirschman's (1970) account of political regimes in terms of 'exit, voice and loyalty' has inspired a number of different attempts to classify the elements in a political order which explain its stability or instability and how external change (such as economic globalisation or cross-continental religious revival) might upset the balance between these and contribute to social disorder.

My own contribution to these accounts (Jordan 2008, pp. 136–9 and *passim*) was framed in terms of *intimacy, respect and belonging*. Although *intimacy* is generally a term used for close emotional relationships and feelings, including sexual ones, it was used by Giddens (1991) to refer to the rise of a form of individualism in which citizens develop 'projects of self', which prioritise 'authenticity' in personal relations, negotiated with others (pp. 75, 78–9, 89, 97). I pointed out that, in the analyses of well-being which burgeoned in the new century (e.g. Helliwell 2003; Layard 2005), intimacy represented a 'warm' element in the social value that constituted well-being, which could easily become overheated, turning to hate and actually depleting this value. Latin American and Mediterranean cultures are commonly supposed to illustrate this tendency and do not score very highly in league tables of national well-being (compared, for instance, with more temperate Scandinavian ones).

Respect is a cooler source of social value; it comprises the recognition and regard which are produced and distributed in public life, including economic activity, civil society organisations, casual encounters in the street, the workplace and the agencies of the state. *Belonging*, like intimacy, is a warm and emotional source of value, related to the feelings and bonds that are generated in teams, groups, communities and membership organisations (ultimately including nations) and which contribute to identity and security.

Each of these forms of value has its own complex code governing interactions and these vary widely between societies and over time. Their respective meanings and standards have been analysed by Bauman (2003) (on intimacy), Sennett (2003) (on respect) and Taylor (1989) on collective membership and belonging, showing how they generate and distribute value, and differentiate spheres of interaction. These are not, like economic markets, issues of costs and benefits, marginal gains and losses; to be hated, rather than loved, is a painful rejection (*negative* value); to be humiliated, rather than respected, is to lose status and reputation; and to lose one's citizenship is a kind of social exile.

In relation to nations, and particularly to moments of crisis in their histories, Jared Diamond (2019) analyses these in terms of an analogy with individuals (their emotional and personal life). He argues that, for healthy adaptation and positive change, they need to reach consensus among citizens that the nation is in crisis, to accept national responsibility to do something about it, build a fence around the problem to be solved, use other nations as models of how to solve it, take pride in their national identity, be honest in assessing themselves, look at their histories of previous crises, deal with national failures, be situation-specific in their response, identify national core values and minimise the effects of geopolitical constraints (pp. 50–2).

He goes on to analyse the historical responses of nations as diverse as Japan, Chile, Australia and Germany to such crises, finishing with the USA in recent years, as earnings inequality has increased and politics there has become more polarised. Each political clan has developed a culture of increased intolerance of the other; their opinions are re-enforced by the TV channels they watch and the social media tweets they read (very frequently, each day). They have become less courteous and considerate; in colleges, academic colleagues and students shout abuse at lecturers whose views they dislike; they participate less in civil society organisations and join on-line groups instead; they move more often, and further, than other comparable populations and they do not keep in good touch with former friends (pp. 329–51).

As the most unequal large democracy (p. 365), as well as the richest, the USA could afford to invest massively in infrastructure and in education, science and technology and health care; yet spending on prisons has grown 25 times faster than spending on higher education (p. 373). Its graduates rank low among advanced nations in their attainments in mathematics and science, partly because teachers have low pay and status compared with other such countries (p. 373). 'While we have the largest population among wealthy democracies, most of that population is not being trained for the skills that are the engines of our economic growth' (p. 375).

Where the USA does spend more than other such countries is on criminal justice (mainly incarceration), the armed services, and health-care, though the latter is very inefficiently deployed by private insurance organisations and on drugs, and the US comes worst in the league of these countries' statistics for life-expectancy, infant mortality and maternal mortality (p. 376).

The USA is a huge and diverse society, dealing simultaneously with a range of issues such as nuclear armaments, climate change and fossil-fuel depletion. But its failure to mobilise a moderate majority to address these, or to cope rationally with the issue of immigration through Mexico, suggest that more extreme forms of the disorder are not out of the question. In view of its world dominance, this raises issues of real concern.

The evidence on whether the traditional order of national party politics is breaking up is mixed. Perhaps the high-water mark of this phenomenon was the European Parliament elections of May 2018. The overall turnout was high, by the standards of these polls, at 51 per cent, and populist nationalist parties did well in several countries. In the UK, the Brexit party won the most seats (28), making gains from the Conservatives, whose tally of 15 seats was their worst ever, and Labour, who lost 8, while the Liberal Democrats (15 gains) came second and the Greens third. Plaid Cymru came second in Wales, Labour third; and the Scottish Nationalists won most seats there, with Labour fifth and the Conservatives gaining only 5 per cent of the vote.

A similar phenomenon was apparent in France, where the new version of the *Front National* (25 per cent) out-polled Emanuel Macron's *En Marche* (22 per cent), and Italy, where the Far Right *Liga* (not for leaving the EU, but strongly anti-migration) gained 30 per cent of the vote and entered a governing coalition with the *Five Star* movement as the dominant partner. In Germany, the ruling CDU suffered significant losses, but it was the socialist SPD which was the main loser, suffering catastrophic setbacks, as the Greens came to have the second-largest representation in the European Parliament, with the support of the majority of younger voters (BBC World Service, *News*, 27 May 2018). In Belgium, the Far-Right gained in Flanders, the Greens in Wallonia. In Spain, the Far Right Vox Party doubled its support in 6 months between General Elections in 2019, partly related to the turbulent events in Catalonia (BBC Radio 4, *News*, 11 November 2019).

If this was something of a high-water mark for disintegrative sentiments and political movements in the European Union, the following year saw global protests and demonstrations peak. By the end of October, the Lebanon and Iraq were joining the ferment of discontent already being manifested in South and Central America, in Hong Kong and some Indian provinces, as well as elsewhere in the Middle East.

In Lebanon, a whole series of failures in public administration sparked a wave of protests. Rubbish collection had become unreliable, housing provision was very lacking, and fires had destroyed historic cedar forests (the national symbol); helicopter firefighting equipment from Cyprus had had to be called in because the local machines had not been properly maintained. The announcement of a proposed tax on internet telephone calls was the last straw.

What was notable about the protests against these failures of an ageing government, made up of former leaders of the religious factions in the long civil war, was that the old rivalries were put aside as crowds joined together to denounce corruption and inefficiency in government. The young protesters railed against members of their own religious sect, as well as others, and demonstrations turned to celebrations as the government immediately announced large cuts in ministers' salaries and in bank interest rates (BBC Radio 4, '*From Our Own Correspondent*', 24 October 2019).

In Iraq, thousands of young Shia citizens similarly demonstrated against government inefficiency and corruption, and the lack of opportunities for the younger generation, high unemployment and the cost of living. Around 150 protesters were killed by paramilitary forces (BBC World Service, *News*, 26 October 2019). Lebanon and Iraq were the two countries in the region which had not experienced revolts during the 'Arab Spring'; they were making up for the lost time.

So, although there was no clear pattern of larger, national units splitting into smaller, regional ones, discontent and protest against the governing regimes in nation states was very widespread all over the world. It was as if it had suddenly become very difficult to govern collectives of this reach (in terms of different functions and services) and scale (in terms of geographical size and diversity of membership). While this did not necessarily apply any less to provinces and cities, where the populations of those also denoted boundaries round particular language or ethnic groups, these features of their citizenry could encourage movements for political autonomy also.

Sustaining Collective Organisations

The argument of this book is that these phenomena indicated a general problem in the mechanisms and processes for sustaining collective organisations in the present era. Whereas the 1970s represented a crisis for those institutions which relied on Hirschman's 'loyalty' processes (state agencies and services, trades unions and labour organisations) and the 1990s saw their widespread replacement by 'exit' ones (privatised provision, offering 'choice' to all but poor citizens, and additional coercion of the latter for the advantage of the taxpaying former groups), the new decade seems to be experiencing the failure and break-up of many of these new, commercial systems and institutions.

The first symptom of this process was the collapse of the overextended banks in 2007–2008, that began with the debt-laden Lehman Brothers. Several of the UK's largest financial organisations, such as NatWest, were bailed out, effectively nationalised and then re-privatised. Some 5 years later, Carillion, an international company involved in the construction, maintenance and (in some cases) management of hospitals, schools, libraries, prisons and infrastructure projects, was rumoured to be in financial trouble; it later went into liquidation and had in turn to be bailed out. It employed 20,000 workers in public services in the UK (BBC Radio 4, *News*, 13 January 2018). A report by the IMF showed that the continued austerity measures in countries such as Portugal, Greece and Ireland were required because the bailed-out banks had not resumed lending to governments and companies (BBC Radio 4, *Today*, 9 October 2012).

Under New Labour in the UK, the government had cut funding to public services and partially compensated for this by contracting some responsibilities out to voluntary organisations and charities. With austerity, some of this funding was cut, to the point where, under the Coalition regime, spending on grants and contracts was reduced by 11 per cent between 2010 and 2013, according to Standing (2017, pp. 113–14), quoting from a report by the National Council for Voluntary Organisations, while those for children and young people were reduced by 18 per cent; all but statutory duties were largely abandoned. Even Kids' Company, whose work was praised by Conservative ministers, went bankrupt in 2015, drawing attention to the risks of entrusting vital services to unaccountable voluntary agencies.

It was soon realised by staff and service users that this was not a cyclical recession, but the onset of a process in which the costs of a radical restructuring of collective organisations and systems were being borne by their employees and the public. On 22 May 2012, the International Labour Office stated that 13 per cent of young people worldwide were unemployed (BBC World Service, *News*). On 31 October 2011, the same organisation had published its *World of Work Report*, stating that 80 million new jobs would be needed to restore employment to pre-crash levels, and only 40,000 were expected to be created, almost all in developing countries. A few days later, it was reported that US median incomes had fallen by 7 per cent from 2000 to 2011 and one-fifth of US homeowners were in negative equity.

But in the meanwhile, many countries had introduced schemes for employing claimants of benefits on compulsory schemes, under threat of disqualification or reduction of benefits payments if they refused these. Research in Denmark and the UK showed that these sanctions were extensively deployed (Haagh 2019a, b), as these 'workfare' or 'welfare-to-work' measures, on the model first used in the USA (Mead 1986) were rolled out. Yet researchers discovered that, of the unemployed claimants on the company A4e, one of the largest such contractors to the Work Programme, only 3 per cent of those placed in the first 10 months of its operation found jobs lasting more than 3 months (Channel 4, *News*, 28 June 2012).

Two years later, the 'Help to Work' programme, introduced to add an extra year for selected claimants after 2 years on the existing scheme, found two-thirds of these still claiming, and so required them to sign on at the office daily, do intensive further training, or undertake 30 hours a week of unpaid 'community work' (very similar to the conditions imposed by courts on some minor offenders). Research on a pilot study found only one in five in employment at the end of this and several leading voluntary organisations refused to participate in the scheme (BBC Radio 4, *News*, 28 April 2014).

So there was mounting evidence that a substantial number of the organisations which had been restructured or regenerated in the new culture of commercialisation and privatisation were either not viable, or had been seriously mismanaged, or were involved in coercive state programmes. But although states rode to the rescue of many of these (to their immense cost, and—for many—not avoiding their bankruptcy), this did not lead to a restoration of faith in the public sector and public services. Instead, it ushered in the age of angry mobilisations by the newly insecure employees of companies including those bailed out, in mass but often incoherent protests; and this anger was then weaponised by populists such as Donald Trump against the traditional political parties and elites, and towards authoritarian and anti-immigrant policies.

Conclusions

In his programme about '*Order and Disorder*', BBC4 TV, 24 October 2012, the popular science broadcaster, Jim Al-Khalili, analysed the history of scientific theory and research about entropy and the order of the universe. At the beginning of the Renaissance, there was still a close relationship between 'metaphysics' (philosophy and theology) and engineering. So for instance Leibniz saw the world as a living machine, containing a quantity of life-force, created for eternity by God. But in his correspondence with the French thinker Papin, he recognised that energy could be captured and heat converted into useful action; the latter in turn considered that it could be harnessed to do the work of 100 men.

But it was not until the Industrial Revolution in England that this idea was put into action, with the invention of the steam engine. This not only transformed economies and societies; it also launched scientific research into the cosmic principles illustrated by steam engines, leading to the science of thermodynamics. The French refugee Nicholas Carnot framed the principle of 'hot sources in cooler surroundings' that led eventually to the internal combustion engine. The laws of thermodynamics were gradually translated into mathematical formulae and explained how entropy involved transfers of heat in irreversible processes. Atomic physics studied these at the smallest scale, including the mathematics of the probable courses of thousands of atoms travelling in certain directions. The whole system went from ordered to disordered states, distributing energy between a larger number of objects; left to itself, the universe would get more disordered, according to the mathematics of things.

Yet this unwinding of the universe could be constructive if human beings could harness the cosmic flow; we might maintain and improve our own corner of the cosmic order. We are now on the cusp of harnessing hydrogen for energy and could eventually even tap energy from the Big Bang; the Second Law of Thermodynamics could supply the means to a new order.

Which of these two processes, if any, is happening to our national polities? It seems as if there is a tendency towards their disintegration, if not extinction, and the same can be said for the unions of states which are our present-day equivalents of nineteenth-century empires. But this is by no means universal and it is being strongly resisted. The outcomes may be 'autonomous' regions or provinces, certainly not fully independent, but having important elements of self-rule.

If so, this would imply that the global co-ordination required for world peace and the regulation of trade might also require new collective bodies for its rules and deal-making; these, too, would not be a radical departure from existing institutions, but could accommodate a greater variety of constituent members, and a larger volume.

All this implies that the populist nationalism which I have argued is a reaction to the disintegration of collective political, economic and civil-society institutions, and particularly to the economic security provided by large firms, pension funds and state social benefits in the post-war period, will be a fairly short-lived phenomenon. If instead it consolidates into long-term coalitions of rival forces, mobilised in opposition to each other, and willing to use threats and intimidation to pursue their ends, then all these societies could quickly become battlegrounds, to the destruction of their potential for harmony, prosperity and the progress of human cultural achievement.

Furthermore, there is survey evidence that young people have adopted ideas and cultural practices of increased individualism, and devaluation of public services. In 2014, an IPSOS Mori poll in the UK found that they believed strongly in individual responsibility; they were against state redistribution of income, and only 20 per cent were proud of the welfare state (compared with 70 per cent of over-65s). Although they were socially liberal, supporting women's and gay rights, and less restrictive immigration, they thought that fees for university courses were fair, and grants should only be given to the poorest students. They believed in the small state and low public spending, and that drinkers and overweight people should pay for their own health care (BBC Radio 4, *Generation Right*, 16 June 2014).

Older people interviewed in the same survey said that young people were being squeezed hard at the beginning of their adult lives, and having to compete in the new, privatised environment of education tests and league tables. Social media encouraged them to cultivate their self-image and disconnected them from their real-life communities.

In a review of the situation of the UK in the wider world since the Second World War, presided over by David Aronovitch (BBC Radio 4, *The Briefing Room*, 5 September 2019), a number of distinguished commentators gave their views. William Waldegrave said there had been a slow disintegration of national narratives about ourselves during the whole of this period. Peter Hennessey argued that there had been the successive impacts of unprecedented crises—about our place in the world, EU membership, the Irish question, the state of the Union, the condition of Britain, and now Brexit. Professor Margaret Macmillan of Oxford University emphasised the relationship with the Commonwealth and with the USA as in tension with EU membership and the failure of British diplomacy to overcome the negative consequences of the Suez affair having lasting disintegrative effects. The contributors agreed on the ground lost during the long negotiations over joining the EU and confusion about its long-term goals during the debates about the Maastricht Treaty and the enlargement into former communist Central Europe. The Brexit debate, like the Irish question, was toxic, and the crisis was now similar to that before the First World War, with fears about the future of our constitutional balance.

This discussion reflected a high degree of ambivalence and confusion among the British elites about the future of this country in particular, and nation states in general, in the post-imperial world; it identified a crisis, without clarifying its nature, let alone its resolution. British politicians, too, were trying to forge new party images and identities in the parliamentary election campaign of November 2019. Commentators noted Boris Johnson's eagerness to attract votes from the working-class electorate, especially in the North of the country, with uncosted promises to increase spending on the NHS, police and prisons, while simultaneously pledging to give tax cuts to the lowest-earning households (BBC Radio 4, *The World at One*, 3 November 2019). A day later, the Resolution Foundation revealed that state spending had just surpassed its highest level as a proportion of national income since the 1970s (BBC Radio 4, *News*, 4 November 2019) and the December election confirmed the success of Johnson's strategy.

But the news bulletins during the campaign also gave evidence of the drastic deterioration in the quality of provision in some privatised services. For instance, children were being accommodated alone on houseboats, or in out-of-season cabins in holiday camps, under the care supplied by one such agency (BBC 1 TV, *News*, 3 November 2019). This was made public at the same time as Boris Johnson's pledge to end the freeze on benefits, which over the previous 5 years had resulted in an average 7 million claimants' households being worse off by an average £526 a year.

In the second part of this book, I shall outline some of the means by which these negative outcomes could be avoided. But in the next chapter, I shall look at how subnational collective bodies, both political and economic, experienced similar processes of disintegration to those of states.

References

Bauman, Z. (2003). *Liquid Love: On the Fragility of Human Bonds*. Cambridge: Cambridge University Press.

Diamond, J. (2019). *Upheaval: How Nations Cope with Crisis and Change*. London: Allen Lane.

Giddens, A. (1991). *Modernity and Self-Identity: Self and Society in the Late Modern Age*. Cambridge: Polity.

Haagh, L. (2019a). *The Case for Universal Basic Income*. Cambridge: Polity.

Haagh, L. (2019b). Public State Ownership with Varieties of Capitalism: Regulatory Foundations for Welfare and Freedom. *International Journal of Public Policy, 15*(2), 153–184.

Helliwell, J. F. (2003). How's Life? Combining Individual and National Variables to Explain Subjective Well-Being. *Economic Modelling, 20*, 331–360.

Hirschman, A. O. (1970). *Exit, Voice and Loyalty: Responses to Decline in Firms, Organisations and States*. Cambridge, MA: Harvard University Press.

Jordan, B. (2008). *Welfare and Well-Being: Social Value in Public Policy*. Bristol: Policy Press.

Layard, R. (2005). *Happiness: Lessons from a New Science*. London: Allen Lane.

Mead, L. M. (1986). *Beyond Entitlement: The Social Obligations of Citizenship*. New York: Free Press.

Sennett, R. (2003). *Respect: Character in a World of Inequality*. London: Allen and Unwin.

Spruyt, H. (1994). *The Sovereign State and Its Competitors: An Analysis of Systems Change*. Princeton, NJ: Princeton University Press.

Standing, G. (2017). *The Corruption of Capitalism: Why Rentiers Thrive and Work Does Not Pay*. London: Biteback.

Taylor, C. (1989). *Sources of Self: The Making of Modern Identity*. London: Bell.

CHAPTER 3

Collapse of Collective Institutions

Abstract In parallel with developments at the international and regional level, there has been evidence that growing inequality and economic insecurity is putting pressure on all collective units, at every level of societies. The promise of the reforms which created a new economic environment, of privatised services and 'flexible' employment, has turned into a threat, and new technologies now seem to intensify the risks to social institutions. This chapter considers how phenomena like the vandalisation of robot-driven cars by angry pedestrians, and the use of artificial intelligence (AI)-controlled machines not fully understood by their operators for diagnosis of tumours, raise radical issues about how collective systems (transport, health care) should be organised in future.

Keywords Social institutions • Solidarity • Collective resistance

It would be surprising if the pressures that have weakened the collective bonds of international federations, nations and provinces had not also brought disintegrative forces to bear on other forms of collective unit, including those by which citizens seek to protect themselves from insecurity and misfortunes of various kinds. This chapter considers the evidence of disintegration in urban localities and rural districts, which have been bound together by more personal links than those which bind nations and regions; and it goes on to examine what kinds of collectives might develop to replace or fortify them.

B. Jordan, *The Age of Disintegration*,
https://doi.org/10.1007/978-3-030-41445-0_3

So the main issue for this chapter is whether there are some other kinds of bonds and ties, and some different mechanisms, that link the populations of these collective units, and enable them to mobilise for collective action, including the capacity to deal with both crises and more slow and insidious forms of economic and social change. In particular, the pressures arising from inequality and insecurity of employment, of privatisation of services for the mainstream and coercive conditions of benefits for poor people, place far more strain on all such solidarities than those which prevailed under the conditions in which post-war welfare states were created. How might these institutions adapt to new conditions and provide the bases for more free and equal citizenship in the future?

The chances of making such adaptations are made all the more challenging by the advent of new technologies, such as the automation of service as well as industrial work (Jordan 2019b) through artificial intelligence (AI). While these are potentially liberating in the longer term (Stayton 2019; Bastani 2019), their short-term effects tend to increase the insecurities and resentments which have provided the support for authoritarian leaderships, especially in the USA and Hungary (Jordan 2019a).

There are a whole range of new ethical issues about the potential of new technologies, especially artificial intelligence. It is becoming clear that it is not only capable of astonishing speed in calculating and correlating; it also has the potential for anticipating the consequences of decisions which far exceed those of humans. The prospect that they may be able to adopt strategies for outwitting their operators is a daunting one, and has important implications for the future of human collectives.

At the same time, there is continued evidence of disintegration in the political life of our societies, not least in the party politics of the UK in the lead-up to the December General Election of 2019. The flurry of abortive and successful bids for electoral pacts was accompanied by scandals and the resignations of prominent figures, contributing to the sense of splintering, and of enduring problems of integration within these collective bodies.

My task in this chapter is therefore to identify the forces which potentially hold collectives together under these conditions, and particularly how they might provide a basis for future solidarity, even against the background of these threats and hazards. Then I shall examine particular conditions in societies such as the USA and UK, to see what is currently happening to these institutions, and how communities have reacted to this.

The Nature of Membership

The first important step in any such analysis is to recognise that, at the level of cities and more dispersed local authorities, and even of certain other kinds of associative collective bodies, there are forces at work among committed, active members which affect more passive and disengaged ones. These have been analysed in terms of 'social capital' by researchers and theorists, but I shall argue that some of the better-known of these analyses have been misleading, as to the nature and effects of these phenomena (Jordan 2008, chap. 5).

Take the example of sport. The collective forces at stake cannot be understood in terms of the economic 'clubs' which are postulated by J.M. Buchanan (1965, 1968) or others in the public-choice school. Sports clubs are not merely amenities for players, and their functions are much broader than competing against other clubs. They also act as social centres for ex-players and regular supporters, and they attract more occasional supporters from their local districts. Unless they had this wider appeal, and unless they also organised coaching and youth competitions for up-and-coming youngsters, they would not be able to include new young players and attract new members over time. The larger the volume of support they can attract from the populations of their towns or districts, the better the performance and morale of the players are likely to be.

In other words, the benefits produced by sports clubs are quite different in nature and extent from the excludable 'club goods' of Buchanan's theory; they are built from being open, not closed. Nor yet are they the same as the 'public goods' available in the sea, clean air and unenclosed countryside—*freely* open to all. They set rules which define the prerogatives of membership and the opportunities of supporters, all alike sharing in a collective solidarity and loyalty with the team, which they usually celebrate over drinks at the clubhouse or the local pub, especially after winning a match.

So these collective organisations do not operate according to economic models of 'clubs', or the political models of associations (which pursue collective purposes, pleasurable, charitable or in the search for power and influence). Instead, they give 'benefits' (of good health and good company, and the exercise of athletic skills) to players, and of participatory enjoyment to members and supporters: they may even give pleasure and pride to those who merely read accounts of their deeds in local newspapers.

Yet, these benefits are not the 'externalities' of economic theory either. For members and supporters, they are exactly what they aim to achieve; for the wider community, they are the pride and pleasure that they get from the success of the team, in so far as they are aware of this. If all this 'spills over' into increased sales in the shops, or more investment from outside, this is an unintended positive consequence, but not an 'externality' for the wider population of the city or district (Jordan 2004, p. 94).

This distinction is clarified by reference to the work of Adam Smith (1759). His invention of the concept of the 'invisible hand' in *The Theory of Moral Sentiments* anticipated its later adoption as the hidden secret behind the transition from aristocratic feudalism and protectionism to markets, trade, and capitalism. He argued that it was the desire of the middle classes to emulate the lifestyles of the rich that led them to spend their resources on property and infrastructure—an unintended consequence of which was economic growth (pp. 213–15). This is what is meant by an 'externality'.

A good example of this distinction, which has sadly again become very relevant to the situation in the political struggle to find a solution to the Brexit conundrum, is the case of Northern Ireland. Madeleine Leonard (1994) conducted research in a working-class Catholic community in West Belfast during the 'Troubles', identifying 'strong network ties … with individuals involved in a host of informal economic activities, including working while claiming welfare benefits, self-help, family, kinship and friendship networks, reciprocity and volunteering' (p. 931). All this was done under the auspices of the illegal paramilitary IRA, who maintained ideological solidarity, and within traditional gender-segregated roles (with women involved in group activities such as jam-making).

After the success of the 'Peace Process', the dominant political party, Sinn Fein, agreed to collaborate in building bridges with the wider institutions of the province, ending the defensive isolation of this district, but forcing many small businesses there to close, as they could not compete with larger establishments to whom residents now had access. Several community workers also lost their jobs. As Leonard commented, this shift from 'exclusive' bonds among homogeneous members to 'inclusive' ones with diverse citizens reduced the benefits of loyalty and benefited individuals rather than the community, as many traditional practices were set aside. These were limits on potentially gainful exchanges, consciously adopted, not unintended consequences (externalities) (pp. 940–1).

Putnam (1993) distinguishes between 'bridging' and 'bonding' social capital, in his analysis of the very different political and economic collective lives of cities in Northern Italy (with their multiplicity of civil society organisation, recruiting a diversity of members), and those in the South of the country, which are made up of members with similar economic and social profiles. Whereas the former produce effects which 'spill over' into a culture of civility and trust (positive externalities), the latter spawn one of criminality, intimidation and violence (negative externalities of the Mafia type). Writing of the USA, he and Helliwell included informal interactions such as barbecues and parties in their analysis of the beneficial effects of 'bridging social capital' for well-being (Helliwell and Putnam 2005).

It is the nature of these gains that has not been adequately captured in either the economic or the sociological literatures. In economics, they are usually attributed to greater flows of information—for instance, local politicians and members of their electorates meeting at games and club functions, and exchanging local news. In this sense, they are examples of Smith's 'invisible hand' at work, but present-day economists are far less specific than Smith about how this operates; and those social scientists, like Putnam (2000), who in his *Bowling Alone* wishes to attribute the 'revival of American community' to rebuilding of 'social capital', treat it as a kind of Ghost in the Machine which is meant to be relied upon, even when the way it works cannot be elaborated.

While conceding that informal interactions can have negative outcomes, when groups with similar social characteristics form tight and exclusive bonds, this not only can fail to help them 'get ahead'; it may, as in the case of the Ku Klux Klan, serve 'anti-social ends' (pp. 22–3). In his later paper with Helliwell (2005), they concede that criminal networks can generate funds to finance terrorism and robbery, 'bad purposes' for social capital (p. 438). But this is not an unintended by-product of 'bonding' social capital, it is a type of collective action which economists would describe as 'rent-seeking' (Buchanan and Tullock 1980, pp. 48–9).

Returning to the example of the sports club, a better example of a negative externality from group interactions would be the noise from post-match celebrations in the clubhouse causing a nuisance to neighbours. But this need have nothing to do with 'bonding social capital' between members with similar social and economic profiles. The club may indeed draw in players, members, and supporters from well-beyond the city or district, with diverse characteristics; those with 'weak ties' (Granovetter 1975) in this sense make just as much row as those with 'tight bonds of solidarity'. A clearer case of a negative consequence of an externality caused by bonding social capital (in Putnam's sense) might be racist chanting by a hard core of supporters, such as was directed at the England football match in Bulgaria in October 2019, which almost led to the match being abandoned.

Conversely, of course, success by sports team may cement bonds between diverse populations, once segregated in (sometimes hostile) communities. Another example from the sport was the triumph of the multiracial rugby team of South Africa in the World Cup final of 2 November 2019. The team was led by a Xosa wing forward, who had been born in an impoverished township outside Port Elizabeth; news footage showed the rapturous celebrations of the present residents there, and his brothers took the film crew in to see the room where he had slept on the floor as a child. During the *apartheid* era, this community would have refused to show any interest, let alone involvement, in rugby, a sport in which the national team symbolised the dominance of the white Afrikaner population of the country (which provided the government with most of its electoral support and the team with most of its players). Now, at a time when the governing party of the late Nelson Mandela, the ANC, had been reeling under corruption scandals, euphoria over the World Cup victory (attended, as in the case of Mandela at the team's 1995 triumph) by the President, Cyril Ramaphosa, the benefits could 'spill over' to contribute to national unity and optimism in the communities of the 'Rainbow Nation'.

Similarly, the Belfast example could be explained in terms of established economic theory. Once the closed Catholic community was opened up for wider economic and public policy interventions, informal exchanges that were exclusive and attacks on other communities by terrorists were redundant, the 'bridges' to other markets and employments were instances of conventional gains from trade and labour markets, not instances of 'bridging' social capital (Jordan 2008, pp. 98–9).

Furthermore, international comparisons of levels of trust cast doubt on the existence and effects of distinctive 'bonding' and 'bridging' social capital. Research shows that trust in fellow-citizens was consistently high in the Scandinavian countries at the turn of the century and low in the post-communist ones; but Northern Ireland came higher on the list than Great Britain, presumably because of high levels of trust in the segregated communities. In addition, those (unemployed, poor) citizens in Sweden on compulsory 'activation' schemes had levels of trust as low as those of citizens in the developing countries with the lowest equality at that time, such as Brazil (Rothstein and Stolle 2001).

All in all, therefore, the social capital theorists who seemed to be offering explanations of how even 'poorly' connected individuals in societies could benefit from the existence of many associations and networks in their cities and districts, turned out to be offering no more than economic theory could explain, or theories which were not upheld by subsequent sociological research. The analysis of the durability and value of collectives at this level requires a different kind of approach. One such has been supplied by evolutionary biologists, whose unit of analysis is not the individual but the tribe. It was the ability of unrelated families to co-operate for survival that gave humans the edge in the struggle for survival, through individually costly but group-beneficial institutional innovations (Bowles et al. 2003, pp. 135–6). Such groups were the bearers of institutional transmission through their cultures (Boyd and Richerson 1985), for instance in establishing norms of food-sharing and conjugal sexual fidelity during the first 90,000 years of human existence.

Collectives and the Social Order

Social institutions impose constraints on individual self-interest, by encapsulating past experience of groups in their rules, thus co-ordinating the actions of members, and institutionalising them as predictable cultural features. Anthropologists have emphasised that such rules were binding and effective only because they were perceived as 'natural', 'supernatural' or 'socially sacred' by our ancestors (Douglas 1987); today's equivalent is endorsement by celebrities. They justified such laws as property ownership and inheritance—in today's market order, some such status is given to individual choice; but the scope is available for adaptation and change in the institutional order of politics and the economy. The boundaries between these shifted in the era of privatisation (Rose 1996).

Between the end of the Second World War and the late 1970s, there seemed to be a consensus in the UK and most European countries about the services which belonged in the public sector, because it was not in the interests of any business organisation to provide them. The economic theory underpinning this was that, because it was physically or organisationally difficult to exclude non-contributors from certain services (like clean air or water), the only way to supply them to the level that was optimal for the economy as a whole was through government agencies (Hicks 1945).

But public-choice theorists like Buchanan (1968) and Oates (1972) drew attention to the possibility of allowing all but the poorest members of populations to select their own quality and coverage of services by paying for them, so long as members were identifiable to providers. This was followed by privatisation of almost all services (eventually even prisons); some were conspicuously unsuccessful, as in the case of the probation service, which underwent two re-organisations in the space of the same number of years, 'replacing one kind of organised chaos by another', as one spokesman for the officers' union put it (BBC Radio 4, *News*, 29 July 2019). Yet both Conservative and New Labour governments became convinced of the advantages of these programmes; other European governments followed the British example.

The priority for individual choice has therefore come to apply to membership of all collective bodies, public and private, but the well-being of societies depends on their rules for membership and their overall coverage; they are still required to overcome potential conflicts, exclusions and isolations, to allow the co-operative creation of social value in relations of intimacy, respect and belonging in society as a whole, for the sake of the well-being of the nation's citizens (Jordan 2008, p. 157). They must also allow individual members to negotiate social value, within a framework that steers them towards resolution of problems and conflicts, though none can be completely successful in this.

The economic model of social welfare, which gained ascendancy at the end of the last century, was a political form of collective action, which drew on cultural and social changes in society, and allowed them to accelerate—China would be the clearest example. In the West, these shifts claimed to have resolved the political stalemates of the 1970s, which had come to be seen as frustrating constraints on growth and progress. Meanwhile, individuals and households had found ways of escaping the restrictions of that order, through strategic access to certain districts with better schools and health facilities, which advantaged their children and older people (Jordan et al. 1994), defying the egalitarian collectivist logic of welfare states. The reformed institutions conferred social value (and stigma, in 'sink schools' and deprived districts), re-enforcing economic inequalities.

The reforms were successful in relieving governments of responsibilities for policies which economic change had made it difficult for them to fulfil. Instead of accepting the constraints of collective risk-pooling, individual citizens were made responsible for themselves, under the rules of the marketplace, acknowledging that they were more equipped to meet the challenges of globalisation than governments were.

Collective Resistance

Like all the countermovements to Karl Polanyi's (1944) transformative economic processes in his history of capitalism, these manifestations of collective anger and frustration were initially unco-ordinated and largely isolated from each other. Although variants of them occurred in most cities and districts of every developed society, there was at first little contact between them, they later began to coalesce into national and international movements. In the UK, there were the large but fairly incoherent protests of 2011, and all over the affluent world; and the much more choreographed demonstrations in Chile, Iraq, the Lebanon, Syria, some provinces of India and several districts of European countries, in 2019—some of the latter over regional autonomy, as we saw in Chap. 2.

But there were also much more local, and seemingly random, acts of group resistance against quite different kinds of targets. For instance, some robot vehicles were attacked and vandalised by citizens, either because, as pedestrians or drivers, they judged them to be unsafe, or because they regarded them as unfair competition to their trades (as carriers, or perhaps even as driving instructors). One such attack was reported in the US state of Arizona, where residents of one city threw rocks at robot cars because they were holding up traffic by being excessively cautious, while Italian drivers complained that they gave no clue to their intentions by hand gestures, and argued that their cities needed to be redesigned to cope with automation (BBC Radio 4, 'The Digital Human', 21 October 2019).

Other innovations were introduced largely unnoticed by workers, even though they had longer-term implications for the employment of professional staff. For instance, AI-controlled machines for the identification and detailed diagnosis of tumours have begun to be introduced in UK hospitals; these will unquestionably displace medical experts in the future, and many other kinds of new technology using AI and robots will have similar effects on professional workers in health and other services in future (Jordan 2019b, chap. 5). More generally, algorithms for selecting staff are being used to replace selection panels (BBC Radio 4, *PM*, 25 October 2019). The whole question of such systems, often inscrutable for their immediate human operators and subjects, raise issues about whether humans are being manipulated for the sake of powerful business or political interests.

But at the same time, there were movements, in specific resistance to such technological innovation in some cases, and more general in others, to resist threats to employment; these fed into the massive protest marches of that year. In response to months of *Gilets Jaunes* demonstrations, President Macron set up 'Citizens' Assemblies' to address their fears about employment and salaries in France in the autumn of 2019. And (mostly on the political right), support for populist parties in the EU had more than tripled in the previous 20 years, with 11 countries having representatives of these in their governments, and more than one in four votes for them in elections (*The Guardian*, 21 November 2018).

Overall, the picture of party politics in the UK and Europe was one of fragmentation following decline in the traditional major contenders. In the lead-up to the General Election of December 2019 in the UK, there were already splinter groups of MPs who had broken away from these. At the start of the campaign, the Liberal Democrats, the Greens and Plaid Cymru announced a pact not to stand against each other in 60 key seats, in an effort to revive the possibilities of remaining in the EU; the moving spirit of this was Heidi Allen, a defector from the Conservatives. She said that this deal would 'tip the balance of power away from the two largest parties and into a progressive remain alliance' (*The Guardian*, 7 November 2019).

In Austria, the coalition between the Christian Democratic People's Party and the right-wing Freedom Party broke down when the latter's leadership was disgraced by a scandal. After an election in September 2019, in which the Greens had made gains, they replaced the Freedom Party in the governing coalition (*The Guardian*, 30 December 2019). This made Austria the fifth EU country in which the Greens formed part of a ruling coalition, following Luxembourg, Sweden, Finland and Lithuania (*The Guardian*, 1 January 2020).

The Brexit Party leader had made overtures to Boris Johnson, the Conservative Prime Minister, for an electoral pact, but on being rebuffed announced that his party would field 600 candidates in December (eventually around half this number). Tom Watson, Deputy Leader of the Labour Party, resigned for 'family reasons', while Ian Austin, former Press Secretary to Labour Prime Minister Gordon Brown, advised voters to support the Conservatives because of Jeremy Corbyn's influence since he had come to lead the party, claiming that support among Jewish voters for Labour had fallen to 6 per cent, and that Corbyn's record was one of backing for extremism and terrorism (BBC Radio 4, *Today*, 7 November 2019).

Conclusion

The reformed institutions of reconstituted nation states have thus come under new pressures during the period of disorder that afflicted larger-scale collectives. In so far as many mainstream citizens no longer feel that their employments, pensions and savings can be relied upon to give them the desirable choices—over districts in which to live, or schools at which to educate their children, or health facilities for their ailments—they join protest movements, or the newly rising, more radical parties of Right and Left. They no longer rely upon either capitalism or traditional politics to allow them success in pursuing their projects for better, more secure lives.

These insecurities have more recognisable impacts on individuals in their everyday lives than the international and national ones examined in the previous chapter. For instance, the closure of rural and some urban schools in the UK have provoked parental protests, as have the closures of hospitals in some towns and small cities. In the UK, 78,000 hospital operations were cancelled at the last minute in both 2017 and 2018, a statistic which fuelled Labour's campaign in the 2019 General Election, though Chris Hobton, spokesman for NHS Providers, cautioned against using the issue for this purpose (BBC Radio 4, *News*, 4 November 2019). There had been an increase in demand for hospital services of over 3 per cent a year, mainly as a result of an ageing population, but also a rise in expenditures on new drugs and technologies, and the contracting-out of services like laundries.

The justifications for cuts in spending and these delays in treatment offered by the authorities (in terms of cost-containment, or the requirements of the latest innovations and specialisms) do not convince the protesters. What they want are public services which reflect their loyalties to their towns and districts, and their sense of belonging together in a community.

So what seems to the politicians and their officials like rational reform for the sake of professional and administrative progress, or rational planning under severe resource constraints, is perceived by local citizens as favouring the big cities and the international capitalist order. What appears to the former as a new and realistic social order brings disorder to the lives of those who use these services. Much the same can be said of citizens who, as shoppers or small businesspeople, see the decline of high streets, as large, international retail chains close down their establishments in these communities.

But in the UK, the polarisation of incomes and differentiation in the fates of districts have had political consequences, above all in the rise of extremism. In the first week of the General Election campaign, a report by Sir Mark Rowley, former head of the Counter-Terrorism Unit of the security services, said that the lack of integration of some minority-ethnic communities into wider society was resulting in an increased recruitment of members (including vulnerable individuals) into Far-Right groups in the wake of the protracted Brexit stalemate. He said that divisions in society gave opportunities for a rise in terrorist attacks, exploiting a climate of extremism; in the previous 12 months, 174 individuals had been referred to the terrorism-prevention programme (BBC Radio 4, *Today*, 7 November 2019).

Policies that promote economic change and the transformation of collective life at the local level are intended to induce people, including poor people, to switch their memberships of organisations or their residence in districts. Research by the Nobel Prize-winning economists Abhijit Banerjee and Esther Duflo (2011, 2019) in India and the USA has shown that they are slow to do so, and do not move far when they move at all. They insist that this implies that higher taxation on the better-off need not mean a flight of such citizens, nor does redistribution cause irresponsible spending by poor ones (BBC Radio 4, *Start the Week*, 4 November 2019).

The wider implications of their research for theory and policy on mobility and migration will be analysed in the next chapter. How the members of such communities can adapt and deal with these changes will be the subjects of Chap. 5. In the next chapter, I shall also turn to the issues of integration and the minorities in developed societies, and how these, in turn, affect their polities, economies and societies.

References

Banerjee, A., & Duflo, E. (2011). *Poor Economics: A Radical Rethinking of the Way to Fight Global Poverty*. Delhi: Random House India.

Banerjee, A., & Duflo, E. (2019). *Good Economics for Hard Times: Better Answers to Our Biggest Problems*. New York: Random House.

Bastani, A. (2019). *Fully Automated Luxury Communism: A Manifesto*. London: Verso.

Bowles, S., Choi, J.-K., & Hopfenitz, A. (2003). The Co-evolution of Individual Behaviours and Social Institutions. *Journal of Theoretical Biology, 223*, 135–147.
Boyd, R., & Richerson, P. J. (1985). *Culture and the Evolutionary Process*. Chicago: Chicago University Press.
Buchanan, J. M. (1965). An Economic Theory of Clubs. *Economica, 32*, 1–14.
Buchanan, J. M. (1968). *The Demand and Supply of Public Goods*. Chicago: Rand McNally.
Buchanan, J. M., & Tullock, G. (1980). *Towards a Theory of a Rent-Seeking Society*. College Station, TX: Texas A&M University Press.
Douglas, M. (1987). *How Institutions Think*. London: Routledge and Kegan Paul.
Granovetter, M. (1975). *Getting a Job: A Study of Contracts and Careers*. Chicago: Chicago University Press.
Helliwell, J. F., & Putnam, R. D. (2005). The Concept of Well-Being. In F. A. Huppert et al. (Eds.), *The Science of Well-Being*. Oxford: Oxford University Press.
Hicks, U. (1945). *Public Finance*. Cambridge: Cambridge Economic Texts.
Jordan, B. (2004). *Sex, Money and Power: The Transformation of Collective Life*. Cambridge: Polity.
Jordan, B. (2008). *Welfare and Well-Being; Social Value in Social Policy*. Bristol: Policy Press.
Jordan, B. (2019a). *Authoritarianism and How to Counter It*. London: Palgrave.
Jordan, B. (2019b). *Automation and Human Solidarity*. London: Palgrave.
Jordan, B., Redley, M., & James, S. (1994). *Putting the Family First: Identities, Decisions, Citizenship*. London: UCL Press.
Leonard, M. (1994). *Informal Economic Activity in Belfast*. Aldershot: Avebury.
Oates, W. E. (1972). *Fiscal Federalism*. New York: Harcourt Brace Jovanovitch.
Polanyi, K. (1944). *The Great Transformation: The Political and Economic Origins of Our Times*. Boston: Beacon Press.
Putnam, R. D. (1993). *Making Democracy Work: Civic Traditions in Modern Italy*. Princeton, NJ: Princeton University Press.
Putnam, R. D. (2000). *Bowling Alone: The Collapse and Revival of American Community*. New York: Simon & Schuster.
Rose, N. (1996). *Inventing Ourselves: Psychology, Power and Personhood*. Cambridge: Cambridge University Press.
Rothstein, B., & Stolle, D. (2001, September 15–20). *Social Capital and Street-Level Bureaucracy: An Institutional Theory of Generalised Trust*. Paper Presented at a Conference on 'Social Capital', Exeter University.
Smith, A. (1759 [1948]). *The Theory of Moral Sentiments*. New York: Harper and Row.
Stayton, R. (2019). *Solar Dividends: How Solar Energy Can Generate a Basic Income for Everyone on Earth*. Santa Cruz, CA: Sandstone Publishing.

CHAPTER 4

Minorities, Movement and Exclusion

Abstract The crises in several parts of Africa and the Middle East (and Central America), in the first two of which minorities have been persecuted and displaced, have created waves of refugees and economic migration from these regions to Europe and North America. The volume of these population movements has provoked a populist backlash, symbolised by Donald Trump and Viktor Orbán. The challenge for the future of all kinds of political and social collective units is how to minimise exclusion and build institutions which are diverse and flexible, in a world increasingly on the move.

Keywords Migration • Mobility • Social disintegration • Political disintegration

There has been no more compelling symbol of the disintegration of states and communities than the TV pictures of lines of fugitives from the shattering conflicts in the Middle East and Africa, snaking their way across Europe to the Channel coast and packed into fragile inflatables to cross to English shores. Equally definitive has been the electoral reaction to these scenes, in the fragmentation of European and UK politics, and the rise of authoritarian, populist nationalist leaders and parties, as much as a result of South and Central American migrants to the USA as in the EU.

B. Jordan, *The Age of Disintegration*,
https://doi.org/10.1007/978-3-030-41445-0_4

In fact, migration has been a policy problem for liberal democracies for many decades, and especially since the breakup of the Soviet Union and its satellites. Irregular migration from these countries, played down by the UK's Home Office, was none-the-less an indication of the shape of things to come when they were included in an enlarged EU (Jordan and Duevell 2002). The movement of skilled and educated workers from Poland in particular (almost 3 million, if all who came both before and after the EU enlargement are counted) indicates the significance of this for the home population.

But it was in areas where there were few or no immigrants that working-class citizens, already impoverished or redundant through the impact of economic change during the previous decades, expressed their anger about these newcomers in the referendum about the UK's membership of the EU. So for instance people in the North-East of England and in North Wales voted to leave by large majorities, while those in London, with its concentrations of immigrants, voted to remain. Those leavers appeared to see the inward movement of these outsiders as a symptom of the globalisation that had made them marginal to the nation's economy.

In reality, migration is only a manifestation of the accelerated movement of goods, money and people across borders that have constituted that phenomenon. Most of those who make such journeys are tourists or the staff of international companies, pursuing the duties of their employment. Yet the word conjures up the image of clandestine people-smuggling and trafficking in lorries and boats in the dead of night; and recent history has indeed been marked by tragedies linked to such undertakings, such as the death of 38 Vietnamese and one Chinese irregular immigrants in the refrigerated container, drawn by the British lorry driven by a young man from Northern Ireland and opened by the port authorities in Essex on 25 October 2019 (BBC Radio 4, *News*).

But such tragedies are short-term occasions for public sympathy, set against the deep resentment and anxiety among some parts of the communities of the European and North American countries over immigration and mobilised by populist, nationalist political parties. Immigration has been a major issue in the increase in recent disintegrative tendencies in the EU, and in the established party political order of its constituent states, with Hungary setting the pace in being governed by a leadership committed to fencing out further incursions from its south-eastern borders and detaining those who manage to get through.

In this chapter, I shall examine the history of this rise to prominence of migration as an issue, as well as the reasons why migrants choose to move. In one sense, the puzzle should be why the movement of people should be so problematic, since the essence of modern economic life is that every other element in it involves perpetual movement of everything to and from everywhere. I shall argue that the answer to this question lies in the exclusion from an appropriate share in power and resources of the mainstream working classes of affluent societies and the exclusion of a growing segment of these from the ordinary rights of citizens (Jordan 1996, 2005, 2008). It has been as a consequence of this exclusion that the presence of 'outsiders', seen as largely immune from such measures, and as taking an unwarranted share of national public resources, has been able to be used by unscrupulous populists to mobilise this resentment.

The Role of Mobility in Economic Theory

Why was free movement across borders intrinsic to the theory of economic growth that prevailed during the era when the USSR collapsed, new nations emerged from its ruins, and all leading Western political parties resisted calls to limit its increase? The answers lie in the (often inconsistent) theories that explained and endorsed globalisation, and which could not supply coherent policy responses to the evidence of growing irregular migration during the early years of the new century, let alone the new flood of refugees which has stemmed from recent disintegration of states in Africa and the Middle East, or the populist, nationalist reactions which this provoked.

In the period after the Second World War and up to the mid-1960s, welfare states were largely unchallenged in their monopolies over the provision of the 'public goods' (law and order, defence, environmental protection, social insurance benefits, education, health and social care) which commercial companies were believed inevitably to undersupply (see pp. 36–7). But at the same time as financial and industrial firms became international in their reach, new technological means for excluding non-contributors from collective provision were being developed. For instance, telephone networks, using such innovations as satellites and mobile phones, allowed those in possession of the relevant cards or codes to access national and international networks at preferential rates of charges.

The key to all the new developments, including those in formerly public services, lay in the concept of boundaries. Just as national borders had become more permeable through the growth of cross-border investment and trade, so too systems for cost-sharing among members of collective systems had diminished in significance, and the collective geographical unit to which they belonged was largely irrelevant; what mattered was the 'optimum size' for that particular service.

But that in turn depended on whether the standpoint was that of the members of the collective body, or the population as a whole, and whether the local, national or regional population was taken into account (Cornes and Sandler 1986, pp. 194–5). It raised issues about the appropriate boundaries for memberships of that body and of borders for states.

Yet political democracy implies 'clearly-defined membership of a collective as a whole' (Bauboeck 1994, p. 178), and political territory (land) is the only factor of production which cannot move. Freedom of movement of people for the purposes of business, study or tourism is upheld by international agreements, and there is an international convention on the rights of victims of war and oppression to humanitarian protection in they escape their home country. But rules about who can work, who can settle and who can become a citizen are the prerogatives of national governments. This is why migration can become the focus of political contestation and has become such a defining issue in the age of disintegration of collective life.

The powerful financial forces which have driven globalisation seek supplies of labour-power and land which allow the most favourable terms for production and trade of goods and provision of marketed services. From the perspective of these forces, democratic politics are potentially an obstacle to their purposes; they prefer systems of 'managed migration' for the sake of a 'business-friendly environment' (Jordan and Duevell 2003, pp. 30–1). But governments must still exercise stewardship over natural resources, for the sake of sustainability, and (especially in developing countries) consider the interests of traditional collective units, such as families, kinship networks and communities. All this helps explain why migration has been central to the polarisation in the age of disintegration between the support for Far-Right, anti-immigration populist parties and Green ones, and the decline in that for traditional Conservative and Social Democratic ones.

The Theory of Mobility and Migration

So the days when welfare states could rely on economic theory to supply a consensual analysis of 'public goods' in welfare states, and mobility was regarded as a feature of a well-functioning market economy, are long past. But as yet, no substitute analysis can take account of all the complex factors described in the previous section.

In the economic orthodoxies which favoured 'choice' by individuals in decisions about collective units, and informed the programmes which adapted the internal infrastructures of states to enable this (see pp. 31–2), national borders were treated as largely irrelevant. The *mobility* of capital, labour and outputs was always fundamental to the microeconomics of production and exchange in the standard texts of the discipline; labour markets were ruled by much the same forces as those for commodities, through the demand for and supply of workers, from nearby or further away. But this was in tension with the principles of *membership*, the basis for the economics of welfare and distributive justice. In the post-war world of welfare states, reciprocal relationships between members of economic and geographical units seemed to be a credible model, but from the mid-1960s, international enterprises, investing in countries all over the world, and especially in newly developing ones, made it increasingly difficult to sustain the redistributive policies which were the basis for social justice.

If there were international collective institutions for distributing the benefits of these processes of globalisation according to the principles of fairness among members of the world's population, this would not in principle pose a problem—but of course there are no such institutions, nor could there be in the real world competition and recurrent conflict between nations. Instead, these *externalities* (see pp. 31–2) arising from accelerated mobility are uncompensated; the unintended, cumulative gains and losses to individuals as a result of growth in international production and trade create growing inequality in many societies, though they do allow many to escape from other, mainly developing, ones. Global social justice remains a theorist's construct—a dream (Straubhaar 2000).

Instead, as greater mobility undermines collective systems of solidarity among citizens and low-skilled workers in the developed economies lose out to millions of these in the developing ones, states also have incentives to try to attract mobile, high-skilled workers from abroad for their most efficient, high-productivity sectors. On the one hand, this leads to a 'brain-drain' from sending countries (Bhagwati and Wilson 1989); but on the other, it also intensifies polarisation of earnings in the receiving ones, and competition between regions, cities and localities within the latter. Many of the phenomena of disintegration in collective systems described in Chap. 3 can be attributed to this, along with the increased variations in the prosperity of residents in particular housing estates. Local authorities in cities and districts can become the 'clubs' of Buchanan's (1965) theory, as better-off members seek to avoid sharing the costs associated with poorer ones' disadvantages and needs.

The theoretical justification for the policies which enabled this polarisation of communities was one based on individual 'choice'; if each citizen took responsibility for his or her welfare by moving to the district with the bundle of (market-supplied) collective facilities they preferred and could afford, state spending could be minimised, along with the paternalism of universal public services (Oates 1972, 1985). But this meant that both poverty and social exclusion, along with coercion by the authorities managing means-tested benefits systems, was concentrated on the members of disadvantaged districts (Jordan 1996). As the impact of the automation of service work was felt, the numbers so affected grew rapidly—most markedly from 2014 (Jordan 2019a, b; Haagh 2019a, b).

Migration Management and Control in Practice

The differential impact of these policies on those immigrants recruited by businesses and state services to fill skills shortages, and those who came without proper status through clandestine entry, was very evident from the interviews conducted for the research project, the findings of which were published as *Irregular Migration: The Dilemmas of Transnational Mobility* (Jordan and Duevell 2002). Previous researchers in the field had been unwilling to undertake studies of this topic, for rather unconvincing ethical reasons, but we were able to interview a sample of such male and female migrants from Brazil, Poland and Turkey, as well as officials from the various agencies responsible for enforcing the relevant laws and regulations and the voluntary agencies offering them support.

We also interviewed IT staff, nurses and care workers recruited from India under one of the schemes enabled by Work Permits UK. They were very positive about their experiences, even though many of them had come to England for higher salaries, rather than because they wanted to leave their home country. The process had been straightforward, and some had changed jobs and accommodation several times since arriving.

These made an interesting contrast with the interviews with migrants from Poland (then still outside the EU), who had entered the country irregularly, but had now obtained 'Business Visas', to set up on their own account. They had devised ingenious, often devious, ruses for making themselves eligible for these visas by showing that they had entered the country legally. For example, one man had gone on an organised day-trip to France with a party, coming back with a new visa; he said that 'everybody does this' (Jordan and Duevell 2002, p. 11). Another said his accountants had written an entirely fictitious business plan for him; he was an engineer with a degree, working on a building site, nothing remotely related to his 'plan' (p. 232).

Staff of Work Permits UK were proud of their speed, efficiency and flexibility; they had doubled the number of permits in 3 years. They favoured giving applicants the benefit of any doubt because businesses were so keen to recruit staff. A well-known firm could expect to get a permit within a week. An HR manager of a large IT firm in India, working in partnership with a UK corporation, said that she got approvals in 10 days and contrasted this with her previous experiences of the cumbersome Home Office (p. 225). A spokesman for the Confederation of British Industries confirmed that business wanted 'to promote a flexible and mobile workforce' through UK employers in the UK having 'the right and the ability to … employ the best people from wherever they are in the world'; and a solicitor said that 'you can get a work permit for anything provided the person meets the requirements of the scheme'. A manager from Work Permits UK summed up his agency's approach as 'if anything we err on the side of ensuring that companies get their people' (p. 226).

All this contrasted starkly with the accounts of members of the Home Office's Immigration and Nationality Directorate, as it was then called, after a recent overhaul for 'enabling economic advantage', rather than restricting immigration from the New Commonwealth countries for the sake of 'good race relations' in the UK (Home Office 1998, paras 2.2–3), as had been the focus before. But it was experiencing a crisis over computerisation at the time of our interviews, and this symbolised its seemingly losing battle to shift towards rationalising the asylum system and combatting 'illegal work' (Home Office 2002, chap. 5).

Almost all their enforcement staff and their managers were based in London at the time of our research, some 500 in all, including clerical workers, for a city of eight million inhabitants. Although many of our Brazilian, Polish and Turkish interviewees had experienced raids on workplaces and houses, these seemed to be consequences of denunciations by economic competitors or after personal quarrels; these incidents did not destroy the irregular migrants' positive evaluation of the freedoms of their lives in London, compared with the ones they had had, for instance, in Switzerland or Germany on their journeys to the UK, or indeed their home country for those from Turkey (all described as 'police states') (p. 172).

Our interviews with senior and middle managers and front-line staff of the Immigration Service Enforcement Directorate (ISED), who covered the boroughs where the irregular migrant interviews lived, and our observations of four workplace raids, showed that they were aware of the strategies for survival of the migrants, but that Home Office policies pushed them towards prioritising the removal of failed asylum over-stayers, few of whom were caught in workplace raids. One of our irregular migrant interviewees had given an account of a raid so similar to our research observations of one of these that it was hard not to conclude that it was the same incursion; in this, several migrants had escaped out of a back door, with the collusion of their employer.

Many of our Turkish (and Kurdish) interviewees had applied for asylum and lived in settled communities, supported by relatives and friends, and the majority of these had qualified to seek employment. However, this employment (in Turkish-owned textile factories and food outlets, for the most part) was insecure, often part-time, and undeclared (either for their own income-tax liability or for that of their employers). Having fled political oppression at home, they now faced economic exploitation, mostly by their longer-term immigrant fellow-nationals. Unlike Brazilian and Polish irregular immigrants, they demonstrated collective consciousness in their accounts, but were largely unable to mobilise in solidarity, partly because some of the other workers were Polish, and too competitive and individualistic to participate in collective action (pp. 135–9).

ISED officers claimed to be committed to removing 'immigration offenders', not merely failed asylum seekers and over-stayers, and used judgement and discretion over removals, in a spirit of civil liberties and minority rights. Denunciations by fellow-nationals among Poles and Brazilians made these tasks simpler: they were also aware of immigrants from Brazil in particular posing as language students, and of some language schools being little more than 'visa brokers', with many students registered but few classrooms or teachers (p. 181). The ISED relied on the co-operation of other agencies for information, but the staff of many medical and educational facilities felt it was unethical to report their students who were not actually studying or working (pp. 202–3). The Marriage Abuse Section of the ISED was the most proactive at this time, and some registrars of marriages took their own initiative in reporting what they suspected to be bogus marriages between migrants and citizens or those with settled status (pp. 182–3). Migrants, however, saw co-operation between the ISED and police as tenuous, often making it easy for them to escape removal. One Polish irregular described a raid in which most of his colleagues without proper status managed to flee, but their boss, who did not have a Work Permit, was arrested (p. 184).

Overall, then, the attempt to regulate 'economic migration' and deter 'bogus asylum seeking' was proving very challenging for the Home Office at the time of our research study. The ISED staff accepted the limitations of their effectiveness, given staff numbers and the administrative chaos at that time. Unlike Work Permits UK, the ISED was working against the grain of globalisation; their staff could not turn back the tide of migration by impoverished (often well-educated) young men and women, attracted by the prospect of higher earnings and undeterred by the risks of deportation.

Our research demonstrated that the sphere of national protectionism represented by immigration controls was inconsistent with the enormous global impetus towards mobility of labour, to match that of capital and technological know-how. These forces had already undermined the integrity of welfare states as systems for regulating the relationships between citizens and the distribution of income shares among them. It was an unrealistic goal of policy to seek to place strict controls on the mobility across national borders of people. Soon after this research project was completed, the accession of Poland to the EU meant that the attempt to exclude migrants from that country was discontinued, while the accession of Bulgaria and Romania a few years later allowed a new wave; by the beginning of 2019, there were over half a million Romanians living in the UK, second only to Polish nationals (BBC Radio 4, *The Romanian Wave*, 23 January 2019).

This is all of immediate relevance because the exit of the UK from the European Union (which was imminent at the time this book was being written) once more poses the challenges faced at the time of this earlier research. The phenomena we investigated in 2000–2002 were still the out-workings of the disintegration of Soviet-style state socialism in Central and Eastern Europe; they disrupted the Third Way attempts of Tony Blair, Gordon Brown and David Cameron to forge a new version of an integrated order in the UK, which combined capitalist market efficiency with new forms of income distribution, like tax credits. But the impact of the financial crash revealed the flaws in these strategies, and the stagnation in the economy for the following several years, combined with the impact of new technology, now threatens the country with the forms of disintegration explored in this book. Immigration is declining as Brexit looms.

Conclusions

The history of immigration policy in the UK is an illustration of how these issues have defeated national government policies worldwide. What are required are measures to balance attracting the high-skilled workers required by industries and services with preventing the influx of irregular migrants. In the UK, the schemes for recruiting doctors, nurses and other professionals for the NHS are vital; a quarter of all doctors were born overseas, and one in eight of all the service's workers, such as chefs, cleaners and night-porters, were recruited from abroad. Yet 60,000 of these would not have been qualified to enter the country under present immigration rules. More generally, the total immigration 'targets' set by Conservative governments in recent years have always been exceeded, as have those for the time taken by the authorities to process asylum claims (BBC Radio 4, *Today*, 7 November 2019).

The growth in migration flows worldwide reflects the disintegrative processes in collective systems in the present age. On 29 October 2019, the disintegration of two very different polities, with thousands of miles between them, was happening simultaneously. In the UK, the parliamentary stalemate over Brexit, which had dragged on for months, looked set to be partially resolved by agreement about when a deal with the EU would come into force, at least in its outlines. But a General Election at the end of the year still threatened to re-open the whole issue, and to afford an opportunity for the parties that aimed for Remain (the Liberal Democrats and the Scottish National Party) to stand for a second 'People's Vote', and the separatist SNP and Welsh nationalists to press the case for their independence, winning votes from the Labour Party; at the same time, the Far-Right Brexit Party could assert its claims, at the expense of

Conservative support, with the future allegiances (if any) of the Democratic Unionists in Northern Ireland still unclear.

At exactly the same time, Iraq was being torn apart by mass protests in several cities, and several of these being attacked by paramilitary gunmen; in Kerbala, hundreds of Shia Muslims were injured and dozens killed. Yet television pictures showed these marches as wild celebrations by young men, more like a dance of triumph. After decades of conflict, followed by misrule, the demonstrators were despairing of democracy, which had brought them no benefits, and wanted their homeland back; the government had lost all control (BBC Radio 4, *Today*).

Of course, the chaos in Chile was continuing, with no obvious prospect of resolution, at the same time; but this did not seem to involve specific geographical disintegration, while that in Syria and Lebanon reflected disintegrations which had occurred a long time before that day. Whereas in the UK and Iran, the conflicts reflected issues over ethnic and religious minorities and mobility (in this case, of refugee migration from the latter to the former, the link between these disorderly situations), the other disintegrations were mainly economic in origin—inequality and poverty, exacerbated by regional factors.

So both the causes and consequences of political and social disintegration were related to mobility and migration, but re-enforced by economic globalisation. Some evidence of these forces at work was on show at the Rugby Union World Cup semi-finals in Japan on 26–27 October 2019. The England team contained several players of Samoan and Tongan origins, while the New Zealand one included immigrant Islanders, as well as Maoris. At the start, during the traditional All Black 'haka' (challenging war dance), the England team stood in a contemptuous 'V' formation, and the captain was seen to be smirking—all of which seemed to unnerve the New Zealanders. England scored an almost immediate try and went on to win convincingly, later being fined a derisory sum for a couple of players straying into the New Zealand half during the haka. In the other semi-final, the narrow victory by the racially diverse South African starting fifteen over Wales was achieved by a surge in the last few minutes by a pack of forwards, re-enforced by an exclusively white, Afrikaner set of substitutes, indistinguishable from the Springboks of the 1970s.

In liberal democratic theory, individuals are morally equal, and it should be impossible to give moral reasons for selecting some and rejecting others for membership or physical survival. Economic efficiency requires mobility, which in turn requires a basic level of health and welfare to sustain it.

Therefore, logically they should be free to choose where to live and work, in order to achieve these standards, and have access to the means of survival there. These standards apply to the internal collective arrangements of nation states and there are no persuasive principles indicating that they should not apply to the world as a whole, especially given the momentum towards globalisation (Jordan and Duevell 2003, p. 129).

This implies that societies, as economies, should be as open as possible, and states should supply collective institutions to facilitate openness. Yet human needs for recognition, reciprocity, intimacy, cultural projects and recreational activities can only be met through common interests in sharing and redistribution among members and membership implies boundaries of inclusion and exclusion. States as membership systems must therefore develop rights and responsibilities of members and rules for interactions with outsiders, including ones for access to membership. But they are not closed membership systems (Rawls 1993, p. 277), nor yet, like civil society associations or kinship groups, collectives with rights to impose responsibilities for contributions (e.g. work obligations), or to threaten forms of exclusion (Cole 2000, chaps. 4 and 5).

This was why the Berlin Wall was seen as a symbol of oppression and injustice. The East German regime was so unable to win loyalty from its citizens that 3.1 million of them had moved to the West by 1961, a fifth of the state's population. The wall stood until 1989, when its demolition by citizens of the East sparked the collapse of Soviet-style communism all over Central and Eastern Europe. But ironically walls—to *exclude* immigrants rather than to hedge in citizens—are now being constructed all over the world. The most notorious of these is Donald Trump's, on the border with Mexico. But the barrier between Mozambique and South Africa, where more people were electrocuted in the three years to 1992 than in the 30 years of the Berlin Wall, and the walls separating the communities in Belfast during the 'Troubles' still stand, in places 50 feet tall, the oldest relic of the history of civil conflict and a barrier to real integration between Protestants and Catholics. Viktor Orbán's fence is proving very effective in keeping refugees from the Middle East wars out of Hungary, an ethnically uniform country which has herded its Roma population into one area; it has reduced access of these by 99 per cent since 2015. Along with the fences built by the Israeli regime, one effectively isolating the whole Gaza Strip, these proliferations of border barriers signal an age of anxiety-induced segregation, willing to sacrifice the universal human rights which were presumed to have triumphed in 1989 (BBC Radio 4, 'Build the Wall', 9 November 2019).

In the next chapter, I shall consider the implications of migration, mobility and other disintegrative factors on the nature and collective life of communities. How can open societies with clear rights to access also nurture the functioning of such very different social formations?

References

Bauboeck, R. (1994). *Transnational Citizenship: Membership and Rights in International Migration*. Aldershot: Edward Elgar.

Bhagwati, J. N., & Wilson, J. D. (1989). *Income Taxation and International Mobility*. Cambridge, MA: MIT Press.

Buchanan, J. M. (1965). An Economic Theory of Clubs. *Economica, 32*, 1–14.

Cole, P. (2000). *Philosophies of Exclusion: Liberal Political Theory and Immigration*. Edinburgh: Edinburgh University Press.

Cornes, A., & Sandler, T. (1986). *The Theory of Externalities, Public Goods and Club Goods*. Cambridge: Cambridge University Press.

Haagh, L. (2019a). *The Case for Universal Basic Income*. Cambridge: Polity.

Haagh, L. (2019b). Public State Ownership with Varieties of Capitalism: Regulatory Foundations for Welfare and Freedom. *International Journal of Public Policy, 15*(2), 153–184.

Home Office. (1998). *Fairer, Faster and Firmer: A Modern Approach to Immigration and Asylum*. Cm 4018. London: Stationery Office.

Home Office. (2002). *Secure Borders, Safe Haven: Integration with Diversity in Modern Britain* (White Paper). London: Stationery Office.

Jordan, B. (1996). *A Theory of Poverty and Social Exclusion*. Cambridge: Polity.

Jordan, B. (2005). *Social Policy for the Twentieth Century: New Perspectives, Big Issues*. Cambridge: Polity.

Jordan, B. (2008). *Welfare and Well-Being: Social Value in Public Policy*. Bristol: Policy Press.

Jordan, B., & Duevell, F. (2002). *Irregular Migration: The Dilemmas of Transnational Mobility*. Cheltenham: Edward Elgar.

Jordan, B., & Duevell, F. (2003). *Migration: The Boundaries of Equality and Justice*. Cambridge: Polity.

Oates, W. E. (1972). *Fiscal Federalism*. New York: Harcourt Brace Javonovitch.

Oates, W. E. (1985). Searching for Leviathan: An Empirical Study. *American Economic Review, 79*, 578–583.

Rawls, J. (1993). *Political Liberalism* (p. 277). New York: Columbia University Press.

Straubhaar, T. (2000). *Why Do We Need a General Agreement on Movements of People?* HWWA Discussion Paper 94. Hamburg: Institute of International Economics.

CHAPTER 5

Communities and Associations

Abstract Communities are collective membership systems, intermediate between associations and polities. The rapid increase in the use of mobile phones and social media, especially by younger people, has reduced the face-to-face interactions on which traditional communities rely. Some of these media have enabled the rise of new kinds of collective action, such as the 'Me Too' movement of women who have suffered from sexual abuse. But the long-term effects of these technologies on communities and civil society associations are still largely unknown. There seems to be evidence that these forms of communication reduce conventional civility and enable insulting and degrading messages; for instance young minority ethnic people in the UK report many such incidents, even from fellow-students on university campuses. All this indicates the challenges for community-building in future.

Keywords Community • Collective action • Digital age

Community traditionally implies face-to-face interactions and a shared culture. Such cultures distinguish communities of this kind from the contract-based order of businesses and markets (Jordan 2008), but also from mass movements (Tocqueville 1836–1839), such as the ones which sustained the rise of Donald Trump in the USA, or the protests about the threat of climate change from man-made pollution all over the world in

B. Jordan, *The Age of Disintegration*,
https://doi.org/10.1007/978-3-030-41445-0_5

recent times. This chapter explores the necessary conditions for community, their social and political consequences and their future prospects.

One issue, of course, is whether communities are by nature exclusive or whether modern forms of community are the causes of exclusions in our economies and societies. On the one hand, they are clearly membership systems of the kind discussed at the end of the previous chapter; but on the other, they reflect very unequal access to the collective goods of reformed versions of collective (formerly public) goods and to the supposed freedoms of liberal democracies.

The status of on-line networks and movements mobilised by mobile phone calls and Tweets in relation to the characteristics of traditional communities is complex and will be analysed in this chapter. Are they substitutes for traditional collectives, or do they serve the same functions in new and more effective ways, including the capacity to organise for political activity at short notice?

Meanwhile, there are still many impoverished communities, excluded from the mainstream, especially in former state socialist countries of Central and Eastern Europe. In these, some of the subsistence practices of their grandparents in the era before the Second World War have been revived, with urban vegetable gardens and micro-orchards. Their situation is similar to traditional communities in developing economies, and they may adopt illegal improvisations in order to fill the vacuum left by both markets and state systems in their lives; they are also prone to the activities of mafia-style intimidation and violence. Ill-equipped for migration to escape these forces, they often sink into cultures of poverty and survival strategies (Jordan and Duevell 2003, pp. 149–51).

This chapter will seek to address these questions by tracing the historical and theoretical ideas about community and their implications for an age of digital communications. It will examine whether these have any relevance for today's world, or for the one that may evolve when the disintegration of collective bodies which has been the subject of this book has run its course.

Co-operation, Conflict and Community

Human beings evolved in small groups, co-operating for survival and joining together in tribes for sharing food and defending their territory or waging war on others to acquire possession of theirs. Anthropological studies tell us that these involved ritual reciprocity to sustain the order of their communities, many institutionalising the giving of gifts and assistance among members unconditionally, known as 'generalised reciprocity' (Sahlins 1974). With the creation of private property and of states with monopolies over its protection, under threats of punishment, these systems were pushed to the margins of societies. Hobbes, who proclaimed himself the first political philosopher worthy of the name, thought that the state of nature was one of war, so reciprocal systems could not be relied upon. Since his seminal work, social scientists have been trying to find a basis for reliable co-operation within diverse communities. They have deployed many theoretical and empirical methods, including computerised games (Axelrod 1984).

With the advent of the new politics of competitive individualism in market environments came theories of choice, but these were seldom convincing applied to the world of politics or community relationships (Margolis 1982). Communities are not like markets and the satisfaction of individual preferences; they involve *creating* the goods of community, alternatively the 'common good' (Jordan 1986, p. 49), by negotiation, debate and compromise, often without calculating our inputs of time and energy to this process, in order to enhance the quality of their lives together.

In the Middle Ages, most economic and social interactions took this form, but in England, the lives of people in towns and cities were increasingly commercial and individualistic (Macfarlane 1978). By the late sixteenth century, this process had gone so far and the peasantry had become so vulnerable to epidemics and famines that the state had to legislate for parishes to provide relief (food, money or care) for destitute citizens. The same processes occurred all over Europe (de Swaan 1988); it was the origin of all public services.

The spirit of these laws and services was paternalistic; but there was an even older tradition, dating back to the *Politics* and *Ethics* of Aristotle during the Greek civilisation (the republican tradition of Machiavelli, Rousseau, David Hume and Adam Smith), which upheld the participation of active citizens in the creation of their own institutions and collective provision. It was this form of community that informed the American Revolution and the political philosophy of its leading theorist, Thomas Jefferson (1784 [1903]).

Recent advocates of community such as Tony Blair in his Third Way and David Cameron with his Big Society saw this in far more limited terms, as a way of justifying less comprehensive public services and the expectation that citizens, including those with the fewest resources of all kinds, should be responsible for their own welfare and well-being (Jordan 2005, 2008). As austerity affected a whole new generation, reducing their access to lucrative and secure career pathways and increasing their liability to high costs such as fees and accommodation for their university studies, young people grew increasingly angry and took part in mass protest marches and demonstrations against governments.

In what sense are these new movements '*communities*'? They certainly lack many of the characteristics used in my definition at the start of this chapter; their members usually meet each other face-to-face only in the sense iconically represented by Facebook. They therefore cannot construct a social order (or disorder) by the processes analysed by Goffman (1967)—the interpersonal building of a local reality by exchanges of social value. And yet this is precisely what such users of social media have seemed to be able to do, and on a massive scale, in the mobilisations for opposition to climate change in 2019, to their overall situations in the UK in the summer of 2011 and for support for Donald Trump in the USA before the presidential election of 2016.

Perhaps the difference between the impact of Facebook and that of older forms of electronic message communications lies precisely in the fact that those who receive messages can have access to each other's faces. It may even be that these mobilisations prove that the means by which human beings can (usually unconsciously) deduce a great deal more than the sense conveyed by the literal meanings of their words (nuances, ambiguities, jokes, ironies or insincerities, as well as the overall integrity, convincingness and social standing of the message-sender) if they can see their face (Jordan 2008, pp. 140–1). In his analysis, face-to-face communications such as those which take place in geographical and associational communities, both claim 'social value' and construct social reality. Indeed, repeated interactions establish a collaborative process of mutual acceptance in social roles which is central to the stable relationships of communities (Goffman 1967, pp. 5 and 7–11).

New Movements, Potential Communities

If social media communications may fall short of the local reality-building described by Goffman, they certainly allow ideas to be shared and elaborated into ideologies, and groups to be expanded into associations and movements. These can then be built into more personal relationships, and longer-term exchanges. A friend of mine who took part in the huge anti-Brexit march in 2019 said that it was a remarkably friendly and sociable experience; he got into conversations with several fellow-marchers, from distant parts of the country and from Ireland, with whom he could stay in contact through social media.

However, so far it has been the 'Me Too' movement of women who have suffered sexual abuse that originated in response to the Harvey Weinstein scandal, which has given rise to local groups of women of all ages in many areas of the UK. It was the social media messages in response to the publicity surrounding that case which enabled the growth of these groups and associations.

By contrast, the Extinction Rebellion mass protests do not, so far, appear to have given rise to other kinds of collective action. In the nineteenth century, agitation for the vote by the working-class Chartist Movement in the first half of that era led to trades union formations in many industries and regions, and these in turn spawned such organisations as allotment associations, sports clubs and pigeon-fancier clubs in working-class communities. It remains to be seen whether the new generation will mobilise at the local level in the present-day equivalents of these and whether social media will play an important part in such processes.

Another tragedy which has given rise to mass collective action in local communities was the Grenfell Tower fire. When a room caught fire in a flat on a near-ground floor, it spread to the supposedly fire-proof cladding on the outside of the 40-storey building, leading to 90 deaths and hundreds of hospitalisations of residents. Those who escaped the fire formed an association to campaign for rectification of their wrongs by this council and the investigation of risks to tenants in other such high-rise buildings.

At the Inquiry into the causes of and response to the fire, the Chair, Sir Martin Moore-Bick, said that the London Fire Brigade's Chief Officer had had no training in how to recognise the need for evacuation of the building or how to carry it out. The firemen who entered the building gave very bad advice to residents in the upper stories to stay put; most of those who ignored this and tried to go down the only staircase escaped with their lives. The change in advice which could have saved most eventually came an hour and a half too late. The staff of the temporary control room were untrained for this task and gave bad advice to those who telephoned them. Lessons from previous comparable tragedies had not been learned. Dani Cotton, the London Fire Brigade's Commissioner, had said in evidence to the Inquiry that she would not change anything she did with the benefit of hindsight. No conclusions had yet been drawn, actions taken or policies changed (BBC Radio 4, *News*, 29 October 2019).

The residents' action group, 'Justice for Grenfell', was very critical of the response from all the authorities. Their spokesperson, Mona Samuels, said that the Council (Kensington and Chelsea) was the richest borough in London, but the most unequal, and the poor residents got 'a terrible deal'. The spokesman for the residents said that there was no meaningful response in the intervening 2 years, cladding of the same kind as facilitated the spread of the fire was still in place on several other towers, locally and nationally, and the fire service did not seem to have learned lessons.

Still worse, it had emerged earlier in the year that the two US firms which were supplying cladding for UK projects like Grenfell Tower were well aware that their product was incendiary and had been blamed for fires in blocks of flats in the USA. They had simply sold it abroad regardless (Channel 4, *News*, 11 June 2019).

This tragedy showed that communities could organise for effective responses, but the warnings they had issued had been ignored by the authorities. The problems lay in the power and decision-making bodies, not the lack of community organisation and awareness of the residents. What was needed was a reform of local democracy to make it less deaf to the voices of communities and associations.

But there was also evidence that both rampant individual and racial prejudice were blighting these very communities and hampering the evolution of constructive community action. The reports of young people using racist taunts, both face-to-face and on-line, directed at neighbours and classmates, were indications of damaging divisions and conflicts. At the end of 2018, it was reported that 4500 boys had been excluded from school for racist bullying, up by 500 from the previous year (BBC Radio 4, *News*, 1 December 2018). The need for a politics which unites disadvantaged and mainstream populations for common, progressive purposes is as obvious as ever.

Conclusions

The examples in this chapter have been drawn mainly from the UK; but there are some even more striking ones from other countries, both in Europe and in developing countries all over the world. They all illustrate the transformation from generalised mass protests to specific collective action groups at the level of communities.

A good example is that of France. In early February 2018, 150 people were injured in mass demonstrations in Paris, including 50 members of the police and security services. The demonstrators seemed mainly to be from groups and communities on the verge of poverty; they burnt buildings and cars and vandalised the Arc de Triomphe. Some 100,000 took place in many protest actions right across the country.

Eighteen months later, President Macron broadcast his response to the demands of the *Gilets Jaunes* protesters. He was setting up two systems for 9300 'Citizens' Debates' around France, involving a 'random selection' of these, shortlisted to 150 participants in each. They would be taken from all walks of life, and across the age groups, and would be fully briefed about the issues to be discussed. One set of Assemblies was to be specifically about Climate Change; the other was to debate a set of issues so numerous and complex that the members would be unlikely to see any connections between them. (This contrasted with the Irish Citizens' Assembly, on which the French was supposed to have been modelled, which dealt solely with the question of gay marriages). The decisions to be taken by the Assemblies were for the French nation alone and did not apply to any other member nation of the EU.

The Assemblies proposal was criticised for its incoherent mixture of issues—for its exclusively national focus, and for the danger that initially widespread interest in them could quickly wane, leaving their proceedings exclusively in the hands of older people with spare time and militants with particular pet projects and causes. However, it is an ambitious attempt at a public consultation in response to popular discontent (*Ouest-France*, 4 October 2019).

At the same time, mass protests were continuing in all the other countries previously mentioned and most spectacularly in Pakistan. There the Prime Minister, the former Test cricketer Imran Khan, faced demonstrations by citizens accusing him of being a puppet of the military, supported by the Intelligence Service and in league with religious conservatives. His only real survival prospects lie in the lack of any coherent opposition strategies for tacking the rapid inflation, earnings declines and rising poverty in the country (BBC Radio 4, *From Our Own Correspondent*, 31 October 2019).

But even at the small scale of local communities in deprived districts of Central Europe, such as those described in the introduction to this chapter, there has been some evidence of new and more hopeful initiatives. In a region of Northern Hungary dominated by iron mining and steel production in the socialist period, the closure of all these plants in the late 1980s had left the economy in a state of rural poverty. An NGO bought all the land in one village at a knock-down price, allowing a local association to divide it into subsistence plots for residents and a collective area for market crops. Unlike associations elsewhere in Hungary, it comprised both Roma and white Hungarian members, separated from each other once the collective life of the industrial phase had been shut down; this became the main economic activity of the village community. It was, ironically, a kind of rural communism, marking a transition from the feudal social relations of the pre-war community, via the failure of state socialism, to capitalist market failure—co-operative collective action by a whole, diverse local community (Jordan and Duevell 2003, p. 153).

Overall then, the worldwide picture, from the months-long demonstrations for greater equality in Chile to the mass protests in Pakistan and Iraq, was one of potential for new social movements and purposeful organisations, countering the characteristic disintegration of the present age. The manifestations of resistance and rebellion were leading to a ferment of new ideas and the possibility of new collective organisations and community projects. At the same time, as national and regional political units were in the process of collapse, some kinds of new integration seemed to be starting at this level, born of opposition to the prevailing order. This will be further investigated in the next chapter.

References

Axelrod, R. (1984). *The Evolution of Co-operation*. New York: Basic Books.

Goffman, E. (1967). On Face Work: An Analysis of Ritual Elements in Interaction. In *Interaction Ritual: Essays in Face-to-Face Behaviour* (pp. 47–96). New York: Doubleday Anchor.

Jefferson, T. (1784 [1903]). Notes on Virginia. In A. Lipscombe (Ed.), *The Writings of Thomas Jefferson*. Washington, DC: Jefferson Memorial Association.

Jordan, B. (1986). *The Common Good: Citizenship, Morality and Self-Interest*. Oxford: Blackwell.

Jordan, B. (2005). *Social Policy for the Twenty-First Century: New Perspectives, Big Issues*. Cambridge: Polity.

Jordan, B. (2008). *Welfare and Well-Being: Social Value in Public Policy*. Bristol: Policy Press.

Jordan, B., & Duevell, F. (2003). *Migration: The Boundaries of Equality and Justice*. Cambridge: Polity.

Macfarlane, A. (1978). *The Origins of English Individualism: The Family, Property and Social Transition*. Oxford: Blackwell.
Margolis, A. (1982). *Selfishness, Altruism and Rationality: A Theory of Social Choice*. Cambridge: Cambridge University Press.
Sahlins, M. (1974). *Stone Age Economics*. London: Tavistock.
Swaan, A. de. (1988). *In Care of the State: Health Care, Education and Welfare in Europe and the USA in the Modern Era*. Cambridge: Polity.

CHAPTER 6

Protest, Disorder and Social Control

Abstract Mass demonstrations have led to violent police action, for instance in France, and now Boris Johnson has promised more police and a large increase in prison places in the UK. All of this points to an increase in both collective action for progressive change, and in authoritarian methods of social control, to deal with the social consequences of increased inequality. Authoritarian regimes have few qualms about using overt repression to impose their versions of order on societies in disintegration.

Keywords Collective action • Authoritarianism • Societal disorder

The protest movements described at the end of the previous chapter are indications of a political ferment among younger members of societies whose economies are experiencing the kinds of transformations analysed in the earlier chapters of this book. With employment becoming fragmented and insecure, and earnings less reliable and adequate, anger at the growing disparity between their living standards and those of older, affluent households has boiled over. So far, protest has been largely incoherent, lacking in ideas, aims and focus, the only real exception being those related to climate change. Traditional political parties have largely failed to engage with these new mobilisations, and the consequence is the sense of drift and disorientation, accompanied by the assertion of social control, especially directed at poor and minority ethnic communities.

B. Jordan, *The Age of Disintegration*,
https://doi.org/10.1007/978-3-030-41445-0_6

So the question for this chapter is what is to be expected from these social conflicts, and how long the age of authoritarianism is likely to last. One of the factors that will influence this is the extent to which governments can promote social control—either in the direct sense of criminal justice measures or more indirectly through the channels of education and employment policies and the sanctions used by benefits authorities (Adler 2016; Jordan 2019a, b; Haagh 2019b)—to hold back more progressive forces for change.

Harsher criminal justice measures are characteristic of these populist regimes, in spite of the fact that there has been an unexplained fall in the rates of criminal offending in all kinds of societies worldwide, irrespective of such factors as police numbers, sentencing, prison regimes or the nature of their political systems and government ideologies (BBC Radio 4, *The World at One*, 19 July 2012). In other words, authoritarianism in politics (including criminal justice policies) followed on from a period of unprecedented decline in global criminal activity.

These trends were paralleled in the UK by the doubling between 2014 and 2015 in the use of sanctions (cuts in rates of benefits, or disqualifications of claimants from receiving them) of unemployed claimants. These included cuts if those receiving tax credits for supplementing low earnings (many of them lone parents) who did not accept additional hours of work, or unemployed claimants who turned down work on 'zero-hours contracts' (Channel 4, *Dispatches*, 2 November 2015). There were half a million such contracts in the UK in that year and they have increased rapidly since then.

So it was the poorest and most vulnerable members of these societies who were on the receiving end of harsher measures of social control. They were also in the weakest position to resist these by conventional political processes, being largely unrepresented in the democratic system; they additionally lacked the resources and skills to mobilise for collective protest. Thus it was understandable that they turned to the 'Weapons of the Weak' (Scott 1985)—minor crime, non-compliance with benefit rules, informal economic activity and so on—to resist these measures. These in turn provoked harsher implementation of social control.

In this chapter, I shall analyse the factors contributing to the long-term rise in these forms of disorder in societies and the recent increase in the intensity and severity of means of social control. I shall trace the former to the growth of inequality and insecurity in societies and the latter to the loss of confidence in traditional democratic politics.

The Nature of Protest in Democracies

Protest movements are an important feature of well-functioning democracies. After all, it was the peaceful protest at St Peter's Fields in Manchester that led to the 'Peterloo Massacre' by militia in 1817, which in turn led to the extension of the franchise and the regulated electoral processes introduced by the Great Reform Act of 1832. Agitation by the Chartists led eventually to the enfranchisement of many of the working class in 1870; and the women's franchise owed its introduction to the protests of the Suffragettes.

But there have also been moments of crisis in which protest has been suppressed or savagely punished. The lead-up to the First World War was one such period; during the constitutional crisis that stemmed from the House of Lords blocking Lloyd George's Liberal budget, which included the introduction of an extensive Social Insurance scheme, there were many different protests, including feminists's mobilisations for the vote and campaigns for Irish Home Rule. The spectacularly unsuccessful bid for a revolutionary establishment of the latter in Dublin in 1916 led to the execution of the leaders, a brutal assertion of social control that had been absent from the British political system for the previous century; in the 'Year of Revolutions' (1848), William Smith O'Brien, a Tory MP, had led a very unsuccessful and quickly suppressed Irish Rebellion and was sentenced to death for treason, but he and the other leaders were eventually banished as prisoners to Tasmania (Sloan 2000).

Protest was, of course, much less tolerated in paternalist late nineteenth-century Germany, a nominal democracy, where working-class mobilisations were conducted under the guidance and regulation of the state; demonstrations for peace and for socialism did not take place until shortly before the First World War. Nazism started as a mobilisation for protest against the harsh terms of the Versailles Treaty, and Hitler seized power when mass unemployment offered his storm troopers the chance to disrupt democratic politics.

So the establishment of liberal democracies throughout Western Europe after the Second World War and the provision of benefits and services (of various degrees of generosity and equality of rights) to all their citizens were conditions which led to two decades of relative social peace (once Communism had been defeated in Greece, and tamed in Italy) with a blind eye turned to the continued fascist regimes in Spain and Portugal. It was a spark of radicalism from the United States (especially via those who had protested against US involvement in Vietnam) that ignited the protest movements of the late 1960s and the whole of the 1970s, starting in Paris, and taken up by left-wing splinter groups all over the continent and the UK (Jordan 1973, 1976).

But with the collapse of the state socialist regimes in Central and Eastern Europe, the courageous protesters who brought this sudden shift set an example to radicals in the West. For example, there were mass demonstrations against the Blair government over the invasion (with the USA) of Iraq, and these took place in Ireland, as well as the UK. So the traditions of protest, and many of the ideas that went underground for decades at a time, survived in some kind of cold storage from one burst of mobilisations to the next, and governments in the liberal democracies could never be sure that their policies would not give rise to street demonstrations on some new issue without much warning.

Yet the mass demonstrations of the past few years caught the political leaderships of these countries on the wrong foot because they had largely failed to counter the effects of globalisation (financial crises, earnings stagnation, inequality and insecurity for the younger generation) which afflicted these societies. As support for the main parties of conservative Christian Democracy and Democratic Socialism fell away, the rise of populist nationalist parties introduced the threat of an authoritarian revival (with the USA and Hungary as examples of its imminent reality).

It was the Green Parties, whose principles inspired the Extinction Rebellion protest marches, which began to seem the more promising long-term alternatives to authoritarianism (see pp. 21–2). Climate-change denial was dramatically challenged by television pictures of the bush fires in Australia, lasting for months in late 2019 and early 2020, destroying hundreds of houses, threatening the outskirts of both Sydney and Melbourne and forcing the climate-change sceptic Prime Minister to return from a holiday in Hawaii.

Sources of Resistance

In the 1970s, it was still possible to mobilise poor people for protest action (Jordan 1973) and attempts at such movements have been made in recent years. Guy Standing (2011, 2017) has identified the growth of a *precariat*, 'consisting of millions of people obliged to accept a life of unstable labour, … many … over-qualified for the jobs they must accept' (2017, p. 28). On the evidence of his considerable worldwide experience working for the International Labour Office, he reports that it is growing all over the world, fuelled by technological change and the casualisation of employment, but that it is becoming more aware of its structural situation in the economy, and that by collective action it can 'force transformative changes' (p. 29). He goes on to analyse the forms of collective action that a revolt of the precariat might best take if it is to succeed in overthrowing the exploitation and oppression of '*rentier* capitalism' (chap. 8).

There have certainly been elements of this in recent demonstrations, especially those in France (see p. 63). But many elsewhere in Europe have lacked focus and specific policy demands, while those in the Middle East, especially in Lebanon and Iraq, have been mainly concerned with toppling corrupt and unrepresentative governments.

Yet in the UK, a new and surprising form of revolt, not involving collective action in an easily recognisable form, still less mass protest, has had some striking success. Gina Miller describes her origins as 'a woman of colour from the former British Guiana', the daughter of a barrister, who brought her up to admire the British Constitution and the Rule of Law. She came to live in London and became wealthy through success in business; but she was horrified by the outcome of the referendum on membership of the EU in 2016, believing the electorate had been duped by false promises, leading to the betrayal of the country's historic liberal-democratic institutions.

Later in 2016, when Theresa May tried to get her Brexit Deal through without Parliamentary approval, she managed to win a case heard in the UK Supreme Court to block this. Then in 2019, when Boris Johnson tried to prorogue Parliament for much of the summer, when the final stages of his Brexit Bill were due to be debated, she again won a Supreme Court case to have this overruled. In a radio interview (BBC World Service, *Hard Talk*, 1 November 2019), she acknowledged that both these decisions had caused 'chaos', but she had used her money and networks, as well as the law, to try to restore constitutional and legal order. Her many enemies hated her for her success in this; some had set up a crowd-funding site to pay a gunman to shoot her (BBC Radio 4, *Any Questions*, 2 November 2019).

Although this story, told in this way, sounds like a lone crusade, it was clearly a type of collective resistance, as she revealed both by her mention of her 'networks' and through the support that she received on-line. It points to possibilities for reintegration in the aftermath of the present period of global disorder.

Conclusions

Disintegration in the present age takes many forms. In this chapter, I have considered the collective and individual activities of members of a new 'precariat'—a much larger section of our societies today than it was in the days when I was an activist in a poor people's movement, the Claimants' Unions (Jordan 1973). But the political systems of the European Union countries have been fragmenting also. In the UK, the electorate, more volatile than at any previous time in its voting patterns, changed its allegiances more quickly. In the election which was due to take place at the end of the year, the Brexit Party sought a pact with the Conservatives, to reduce the effects of competition between the two parties seeking to leave the EU; they were rebuffed. Labour would not seek alliances with other parties (BBC Radio 4, *World at One*, 30 October 2019). A week later, the Liberal Democrats, Greens and Plaid Cymru announced their pact, agreeing not to oppose each other in 60 seats (see pp. 21–2).

Meanwhile, Austria seemed to have become the first European country in which a Far-Right populist party (the Freedom Party), having been included in a coalition government with the Conservatives after a successful election result, saw a reversal of this process as it lost ground following a media scandal involving its leader (see pp. 21–2).

Other developments in more distant countries were ambiguous. In China, beset by the continued unrest and separatist pressures in Hong Kong and continuing to coral its dissident Muslim populations in its Western provinces, the regime seemed to be reaching a serene *modus vivendi* with its Han Buddhist devotees, including the monks of its mountain region temples, founded 1500 years ago. These have become used to visitors requesting blessings to improve their chances of success in gambling casinos. The monks thrive to old age on meditation, gardening and relaxation exercises; the government favours them over their more proactive Christian, as well as their Muslim citizens (BBC Radio 4, *From Our Own Correspondent*, 31 October 2019). Was this a demonstration that the regime was keen to reward those faiths which favour integration, including the one giving blessings to the most avid adherents to the new culture of consumerism?

Extinction Rebellion is a mass mobilisation over Climate Change not obviously related to the authoritarian tendencies in polities, but it has come up against the state's agencies for social control in the UK. Its lawyers have brought a court case against the police for their actions against one of the protests (in the week of 14 October 2019). A police superintendent had had issued an order under section 14 of the 1986 Public Order Act, banning all the protesters' actions in London that week. But the court's two judges decided that this was illegal because the order was meant to be specific, not general, and the superintendent was not present at each of the assemblies to which he applied the order.

As the police considered how to respond to this judgement, hundreds of Extinction Rebellion protesters who had been arrested were planning to sue the Metropolitan Police for false imprisonment. George Monbiot, the author and journalist, who was one of those arrested, described the police actions as 'draconian and over the top' (*The Guardian*, 7 November 2019, p. 4). The Mayor of London, Sadiq Khan, said he had had misgivings about how the police responded to the demonstrations (ibid.). The whole incident indicated that the present culture of social control in the UK has led to a potential imbalance between this and democratic freedoms.

In the final chapter, I shall consider possibilities of more systematic reforms to achieve an economic order consistent with political and social integration and a future of democracy and freedom.

References

Adler, M. (2016). A New Leviathan: Benefits Sanctions in the Twenty-First Century. *Journal of Law and Society, 43*(2), 195–227.

Haagh, L. (2019b). Public State Ownership with Varieties of Capitalism: Regulatory Foundations for Welfare and Freedom. *International Journal of Public Policy, 15*(2), 153–184.

Jordan, B. (1973). *Paupers: The Making of the New Claiming Class*. London: Routledge and Kegan Paul. (Republished 2019).

Jordan, B. (1976). *Freedom and the Welfare State*. London: Routledge and Kegan Paul. (Republished 2019).

Jordan, B. (2019a). *Authoritarianism and How to Counter It*. London: Palgrave Macmillan.

Jordan, B. (2019b). *Automation and Human Solidarity*. London: Palgrave Macmillan.

Scott, J. C. (1985). *Weapons of the Weak: Everyday Forms of Peasant Resistance*. New Haven, CT: Yale University Press.

Sloan, R. (2000). *William Smith O'Brien and the Young Ireland Rebellion of 1848*. Dublin: Four Courts Press.

Standing, G. (2011). *The Precariat: The New Dangerous Class*. London: Bloomsbury.

Standing, G. (2017). *The Corruption of Capitalism: Why Rentiers Thrive and Work Does Not Pay*. London: Biteback Publishing.

CHAPTER 7

Conclusions

Abstract This book identifies a wide range of issues concerning forms of disintegration in collective bodies and their implications for economies and societies. In this concluding chapter, some measures that might combat the threats posed both by disintegration and by authoritarian and oppressive responses to it are explored. In particular, the potential contribution of the unconditional Universal Basic Income, as a measure to reduce coercion by state authorities as the full impact of technological change on employment is felt, and as enabling citizens' future equality and freedom, is analysed in some detail.

Keywords Disintegration • Universal Basic Income • Equality of status

In his book *Upheaval: How Nations Cope with Crisis and Change* (2019), Jared Diamond analyses a series of national crises in countries all over the world, from Finland after the Second World War to Australia and the USA in more recent times, using the analogy of psychological breakdowns and crises for individuals. But what if many such national crises are happening simultaneously in every corner of the planet, and all are experiencing processes of internal disintegration in their collective lives?

This book has examined the present situation from the standpoint of a universal process of this kind and used analogies with the scientific force of entropy. This seems to require (like entropy itself) some coherent

B. Jordan, *The Age of Disintegration*,
https://doi.org/10.1007/978-3-030-41445-0_7

counter-force if it is not to lead to continuous disintegration, and in this final chapter I shall look for some measures which might serve these purposes.

The argument of this book has sought to show that disintegration has recently been the dominant force in the collective life of societies all over the world and that there is little evidence that this tendency will be spontaneously reversed in the foreseeable future. This applies to most institutions within societies, as well as relationships between them. So the task of this chapter is to seek principles and policies to be implemented, against this tide, to counteract disintegration for the sake of a new, more promising, order.

These threats remain nebulous for many mainstream citizens in affluent societies; they perceive the disruption as stemming from the actions of restless young people and irresponsible members of an ignorant and envious underclass. Paradoxically, many of them join support for authoritarian politicians who have been able to mobilise some members of the 'precariat' also.

In some ways, the spirit of the age has been captured by two films directed by Ken Loach. The first, *I, Daniel Blake*, depicted the fate of those trapped in a maze of benefit claims, with bureaucratic delays and punitive penalties. The latest, recent one, *Sorry We Missed You*, deals with the destructive consequences of an economy of low-paid, insecure and variable employments for the lives of households which rely on them for their incomes and the stability of their relationships. They convey how both these features of present-day economies impact the smallest-scale units of our societies, households, kinship and friendship networks and neighbourhood communities.

Some clues about the kinds of collective action which might counter these economic forces in societies have been given in the previous chapter. But the long-term hopes for the introduction of measures to enable more such adaptations and mobilisations lie in politics; they require the reversal of the authoritarian wave and the adoption of ideas which have been explored by many theorists with international perspectives, such as Philippe Van Parijs (1995) and Guy Standing (2017), and piloted in countries as diverse as Namibia, Mongolia, Finland, the Netherlands and Scotland.

It seems that each national government will be faced with a choice between a regime of increased means-tested supplementation of low-paid, insecure and part-time work, as automation of service employment tasks complements that of industrial employment (Jordan 2019b), and introducing a new system of unconditional, Universal Basic Incomes (UBIs) for all citizens (Haagh 2019a, b; Jordan 2019a, b), which will give them a degree of security for the pursuit of education, training, employment and every other individual or collective project.

This choice will be made against a background of political landscapes now being redesigned to enable globalisation, including the mobility of labour. All the forces at work tend towards material inequalities, both within and between nations; but the most relevant contribution of the UBI will be to freedoms of all kinds.

Pilot Studies and Experiments

When the early advocates of UBI (like myself) first started writing about it, we could not have imagined that it would be pioneered in Alaska, Namibia and Mongolia. But what these countries have in common is unexpected access to mineral wealth (oil and coal gas in particular), and the presence of populations of indigenous peoples (Inuits, horsemen of the steppes and desert hunter-gatherers), still spearing seals through ice-holes, herding yaks across the plains and pursuing kudu and antelopes through persistence chases over great distances. The aim of all the pilot projects was to distribute some of the newfound wealth in ways that would do the least damage to their ways of life but give them some security in a time of rising prices in the mainstream economy.

In other words, the UBI aimed at equality of status, liberty and opportunity rather than incomes, and at protecting cultures and communities as much as household standards of living. There were clearly always going to be some different issues in transferring this model into affluent welfare states amongst which only Finland has a comparable indigenous group (Sami reindeer breeders).

So it is especially interesting to see the experimental pilots in super-rich California, sponsored by billionaire Elon Musk. There too, of course, is great inequality, but not so much divergence between the lives and aspirations of the rich and the poor. The issues at stake there, and in cities like Glasgow, which have undertaken similar pilots (none of which is strictly a UBI), concern incentives to do paid work or voluntary activity, and the effects on household relationships (as women get a source of independent income they may not have had before).

Before turning to the evidence available so far, I shall set out the aims and claims of UBI's advocates, so that these can be tested against the available reports (still essentially provisional, because of the still-short time-lapse) of outcomes so far.

What UBI Is Claimed to Achieve and to Counter

Not all advocates of UBI would subscribe to Van Parijs's priority for 'real freedom for all', but most would certainly support the aim of ending the coercion which is explicit in systems like means-tested tax credits and Universal Credit in the UK. It is the unconditionality as well as the universality of UBI that distinguishes it from selective poverty-relief and allows advocates to argue that it alone secures equality of *citizenship* among members of increasingly diverse populations. This implies equal opportunities to contribute, to co-operate, to associate and to celebrate in leisure activities and cultural events—to be active or passive in societies in ways at present reserved for those living on retirement pensions.

In this sense, UBI is like what used to be called Child Allowances in the UK, except that it also goes to each adult member of households. In order to be affordable, it also would replace some or all of the allowances against income tax that go to employees. But it is unlike Family Income Supplements, which are 'targeted' at poor people and withdrawn as their income increases.

This gives all citizens equality of status at the same time as the freedoms which Van Parijs prizes. It does not override other sources of oppression and domination, such as sexism and racism, but it makes it far less possible for these attitudes to be converted into economic coercion. Van Parijs (1989) said that it allowed 'A Revolution in Class Theory' and even concluded that it justified restricted migration in order to allow a just distribution of income and resources (1992, p. 164).

Although the UK Labour Party leadership has flirted with the proposal, in the present world of economic turmoil and authoritarian political responses there has been little opportunity for long-term thinking or planning for the changes which new technologies and climate change will soon require—a shift from what is often demeaning and/or unproductive employment, arising from the demand for obsequious service for the rich or the production of unnecessary luxury goods, to projects for environmental sustainability and cultural development.

All these would require a wide range of policy measures to complement the UBI, and which would need political mobilisations specific to their goals. In other words, the UBI is not a sufficient condition for the good society, but it is a necessary one. Political and human rights are goals which have in past been sacrificed for the sake of economic or social goals, as in the history of state socialism, but we do have the history of this to help avoid it. What is sure is that none of these values can be successfully achieved if market distributions and conditional benefits systems continue to be the dominant features of our economic landscapes.

Conclusions

This book has sought to analyse the nature and consequences of identifiable processes of disintegration in societies of all kinds and in their constituent institutions and organisations. It is not a new phenomenon in history, and there have been other times, such as the religious transformations which engulfed Europe in the sixteenth and seventeenth centuries, which saw similar disintegrations, and which were accompanied by violent conflicts. While there are again religious divisions feeding the conflicts in the present world, especially from the Middle East, at least the continents of Europe and the Americas are experiencing these as terrorism by tiny minorities, rather than civil wars between great parts of their populations. But conflicts can grow, and it is important to diagnose their underlying causes and take steps to address them.

In many developing countries, there are still big issues about how their political institutions will emerge from processes of rapid economic change. As long as the classic capitalist formula for rapid growth is working, poor people from the peasant, rural districts will migrate into large urban settlements and earn higher incomes, even if they have to suffer squalor, overcrowding and lack of public services in their domestic lives and neighbourhoods. But what is uncertain is how reliable these processes will continue to be, and how many of their populations will avail themselves of improved and cheaper transport systems to migrate to the developed world, adding to unresolved social policy issues there and making the proposals reviewed above more difficult to implement and the opportunities for authoritarian nationalist politics greater.

Yet it is important to have models for alternative societies available, so that such populist and opportunist leaders cannot represent the situation as inevitably demanding solutions that are coercive and oppressive. I have tried to give an account of some hopeful indications for the future, as well as ominous ones, and clear proposals on how the worst outcomes could be avoided.

This is the third book I have written for this series this year, and together they form a kind of trilogy, about authority (Jordan 2019a), automation (Jordan 2019b) and disintegration respectively. I have tried to give a balanced account of the negative and positive consequences of change and how the former can be minimised. As the French political philosopher David Djaiz puts it, 'Nous devons trouver un moyen de civiliser a nouveau le capitalisme' (we must find a new way to tame capitalism), (*Le Monde*, 31 December 2019). He summarised his argument in the words 'the reining-in of democracy lies in a simple formula: substitute more-or-less constraining disciplinary rules for democratic deliberation'. To explain this outcome and explore possible ways to overcome it have been my purposes in this book.

References

Diamond, J. (2019). *Upheaval: How Nations Cope with Crisis and Change.* London: Allen Lane.

Haagh, L. (2019a). *The Case for Universal Basic Income.* Cambridge: Polity.

Haagh, L. (2019b). Public State Ownership with Varieties of Capitalism: Regulatory Foundations for Welfare and Freedom. *International Journal of Public Policy, 15*(2), 153–184.

Jordan, B. (2019a). *Authoritarianism and How to Counter It.* London: Palgrave Macmillan.

Jordan, B. (2019b). *Automation and Human Solidarity.* London: Palgrave Macmillan.

Standing, G. (2017). *The Corruption of Capitalism: Why Rentiers Thrive and Work Does Not Pay.* London: Biteback Publishing.

Van Parijs, P. (1989). A Revolution in Class Theory. *Politics and Society, 15*, 453–484.

Van Parijs, P. (1992). Commentary: Citizenship Exploitation, Unequal Exchange and the Breakdown of Popular Sovereignty. In B. Barry & R. E. Goodin (Eds.), *Free Movement: Ethical Issues in the Transmigration of People and Money* (pp. 155–166). University Park, PA: Pennsylvania University Press.

Van Parijs, P. (1995). *Real Freedom for All: What (IF Anything) Can Justify Capitalism?* Oxford: Clarendon Press.

References

Adler, M. (2016). A New Leviathan: Benefits Sanctions in the Twenty-First Century. *Journal of Law and Society, 43*(2), 195–227.

Avery, J. S. (2003). *Information Theory and Evolution.* London and Singapore: World Scientific Publishing Company.

Avery, J. S. (2017). *Civilization's Crisis: A Set of Linked Challenges.* London and Singapore: World Scientific Publishing Company.

Axelrod, R. (1984). *The Evolution of Co-operation.* New York: Basic Books.

Banerjee, A., & Duflo, E. (2011). *Poor Economics: A Radical Rethinking of the Way to Fight Global Poverty.* Delhi: Random House.

Banerjee, A., & Duflo, E. (2019). *Good Economics for Hard Time: Better Answers to Our Biggest Problems.* New York: Random House.

Bauboeck, R. (1994). *Transnational Citizenship: Membership and Rights in International Migration.* Aldershot: Edward Elgar.

Bauman, Z. (2003). *Liquid Love: On the Frailty of Human Bonds.* Cambridge: Polity.

Bhagwati, J. N., & Wilson, J. D. (1989). *Income Taxation and International Mobility.* Cambridge, MA: MIT Press.

Bowles, S., Choi, J.-K., & Hopfensitz, A. (2003). The Co-evolution of Individual Behaviour and Social Institutions. *Journal of Theoretical Biology, 33*, 135–147.

Boyd, R., & Richerson, P. J. (1985). *Culture and the Evolutionary Process.* Chicago: Chicago University Press.

Buchanan, J. M. (1965). An Economic Theory of Clubs. *Economica, 32*, 1–14.

Buchanan, J. M. (1968). *The Demand and Supply of Public Goods.* Chicago: Rand McNally.

Buchanan, J. M., & Tullock, G. (1980). *Towards a Theory of a Rent-Seeking Society.* Ann Arbor, MI: University of Michigan Press.

B. Jordan, *The Age of Disintegration*,
https://doi.org/10.1007/978-3-030-41445-0

Cole, P. (2000). *Philosophies of Exclusion: Liberal Political Theory and Immigration*. Edinburgh: Edinburgh University Press.

Cornes, A., & Sandler, T. (1986). *The Theory of Externalities, Public Goods and Club Goods*. Cambridge: Cambridge University Press.

Daly, H. C. (1991). *The Steady-State Economy*. Washington, DC: Island Press.

Diamond, J. (2019). *Upheaval: How Nations Cope with Crisis and Change*. London: Allen Lane.

Douglas, M. (1987). *How Institutions Think*. London: Routledge and Kegan Paul.

Giddens, A. (1991). *Modernity and Self-Identity: Self and Society in the Late Modern Age*. Cambridge: Polity.

Goffman, E. (1967). On Face Work: An Analysis of Ritual Elements in Interaction. In *Interaction Ritual: Essays in Face-to-Face Behaviour* (pp. 1–46). New York: Doubleday Anchor.

Haagh, L. (2019a). *The Case for Universal Basic Income*. Cambridge: Polity.

Haagh, L. (2019b). Public State Ownership with Varieties of Capitalism: Regulatory Foundations for Welfare and Freedom. *International Journal of Public Policy, 15*(1), 153–184.

Helliwell, J. F. (2003). How's Life? Combining Individual and National Variables to Explain Subjective Well-Being. *Economic Modelling, 20*, 331–360.

Hirschman, A. O. (1970). *Exit, Voice and Loyalty: Responses to Decline in Firms, Organizations and States*. Cambridge, MA: Harvard University Press.

Home Office. (1998). *Fairer, Faster, and Firmer: A Modern Approach to Immigration and Asylum*. Cm 4018. London: Stationery Office.

Home Office. (2000). *Secure Borders, Safe Haven: Integration with Diversity in Modern Britain*. (White Paper). London: Stationery Office.

Jefferson, T. (1784). Notes on Virginia. In A. Lipscombe (Ed.), *The Works of Thomas Jefferson*. Washington, DC: Jefferson Memorial Association. (1903).

Jordan, B. (1973). *Paupers: The Making of the New Claiming Class*. London: Routledge and Kegan Paul.

Jordan, B. (1976). *Freedom and the Welfare State*. London: Routledge and Kegan Paul.

Jordan, B. (1996). *A Theory of Poverty and Social Exclusion*. Cambridge: Polity.

Jordan, B. (2004). *Sex, Money and Power: The Transformation of Collective Life*. Cambridge: Polity.

Jordan, B. (2005). *Social Policy for the Twenty-First Century: Big Issues, New Perspectives*. Cambridge: Polity.

Jordan, B. (2008a). *Welfare and Well-Being: Social Value in Public Policy*. Bristol: Policy Press.

Jordan, B., James, S., Kay, H., & Redley, M. (1992). *Trapped in Poverty? Labour Market Decisions in Low-Income Households*. London: Routledge.

Jordan, B., Redley, M., & James, S. (1994). *Putting the Family First: Identities, Decisions, Citizenship*. London: UCL Press.

Jordan, B. (2008b). *Welfare and Well-Being: Social Value in Public Policy*. Cambridge: Polity.
Jordan, B. (2019a). *Authoritarianism and How to Counter It*. London: Palgrave Macmillan.
Jordan, B. (2019b). *Automation and Human Solidarity*. London: Palgrave Macmillan.
Jordan, B., & Duevell, F. (2002). *Irregular Migration: The Dilemmas of Transnational Mobility*. Cheltenham: Edward Elgar.
Jordan, B., & Duevell, F. (2003). *Migration: The Boundaries of Equality and Justice*. Cambridge: Polity.
Layard, R. (2005). *Happiness: Lessons from a New Science*. London: Allen Lane.
Macfarlane, A. (1978). *The Origins of English Individualism: The Family, Property and Social Transition*. Oxford: Blackwell.
Mann, M. (1980). State and Society, 1130–1815: An Analysis of English State Finances. In M. Zeitlin (Ed.), *Political Power and State Theory*. Delhi: Jai Press.
Margolis, H. (1982). *Selfishness, Altruism and Rationality: A Theory of Social Choice*. Cambridge: Cambridge University Press.
Mead, L. M. (1986). *Beyond Entitlement: The Social Obligations of Citizenship*. New York: Free Press.
Oates, W. E. (1972). *Fiscal Federalism*. New York: Harcourt Brace Jovanovitch.
Oates, W. E. (1985). Searching for Leviathan: An Empirical Study. *American Economic Review, 79*, 578–583.
Polanyi, K. (1944). *The Great Transformation: The Political and Economic Origins of Our Times*. Boston: Beacon Press.
Putnam, R. D. (1993). *Making Democracy Work: Civic Traditions in Modern Italy*. Princeton, NJ: Princeton University Press.
Putnam, R. D. (2000). *Bowling Alone: The Collapse and Revival of American Community*. New York: Simon & Schuster.
Rawls, J. (1993). *Political Liberalism*. New York: Columbia University Press.
Revenko, A. (1997). *Poor Strata of the Population in Ukraine*. Paper Presented at Third International Conference on Social Problems, 'Social History of Poverty in Central Europe'. Lodz, Poland, December 3–6.
Roegen, N. G. (1971). *The Entropy Law and Economic Progress*. Cambridge, MA: Harvard University Press.
Rothstein, B., & Stolle, D. (2001, September 15–20). *Social Capital and Street-Level Bureaucracy: An Institutional Theory of Generalised Trust*. Paper Presented at a Conference on 'Social Capital', Exeter University.
Sahlins, M. (1974). *Stone Age Economics*. London: Tavistock.
Schroedinger, A. (1944). *What Is Life?* Cambridge: Cambridge University Press.
Scott, J. C. (1985). *Weapons of the Weak: Everyday Forms of Peasant Resistance*. New Haven, CT: Yale University Press.

Sennett, R. (2003). *Respect: Character in a World of Inequality*. London: Allen and Unwin.

Sloan, R. (2000). *William Smith O'Brien and the Young Ireland Rebellion of 1848*. Dublin: Four Courts Press.

Smith, A. (1759 [1948]). The Theory of Moral Sentiments. In H. W. Schneider (Ed.), *Adam Smith's Moral and Political Philosophy*. London: Harper.

Soddy, F. (1926). *Wealth, Virtual Wealth and Debt*. London: Allen and Unwin.

Spruyt, H. (1970). *The Sovereign State and Its Competitors: An Analysis of Systems Change*. Princeton, NJ: Princeton University Press.

Standing, G. (2011). *The Precariat: The New Dangerous Class*. London: Bloomsbury.

Standing, G. (2017). *The Corruption of Capitalism: Why Rentiers Thrive and Work Does Not Pay*. London: Biteback Publications.

Stayton, R. (2019). *Solar Dividends: How Solar Energy Can Generate a Basic Income for Everyone on Earth*. Santa Cruz, CA: Chronos.

Straubhaar, T. (2000). *Why Do We Need a General Agreement on Movement of People?* HWWA Discussion Paper 94. Hamburg: Hamburg Institute of International Economics.

Swaan, A. de. (1988). *In Care of the State: Health Care, Education and Welfare in Europe and the USA in the Modern Era*. Cambridge: Polity.

Taylor, C. (1989a). *Sources of Self: The Making of Modern Identity*. London: Bell.

Taylor, M. (1989b). *Community, Anarchy and Liberty*. Cambridge: Cambridge University Press.

Van Parijs, P. (1989). A Revolution in Class Theory. *Politics and Society, 15*, 453–484.

Van Parijs, P. (1992). Commentary: Citizenship Exploitation, Unequal Exchange and the Breakdown of Popular Sovereignty. In B. Barry & R. E. Goodin (Eds.), *Free Movement: Ethical Issues in the Transmigration of People and Money* (pp. 255–266). University Park, PA: Pennsylvania University Press.

Van Parijs, P. (1995). *Real Freedom for All: What (IF Anything) Can Justify Capitalism?* Oxford: Clarendon Press.

Varoufakis, Y. (2016). *And the Weak Suffer What They Must? Europe, Austerity and the Threat to Global Security*. London: Bodley Head.

Index

B. Jordan, *The Age of Disintegration*,
https://doi.org/10.1007/978-3-030-41445-0

CPI Antony Rowe
Eastbourne, UK
March 25, 2020